FROM REALITY TO VIRTUALITY
A SMOOTH PATH TO VIRTUAL SUCCESS

DR. ZVI TUBUL-LAVY

ABOUT THE AUTHOR

Dr. Zvi Tubul-Lavy, born in 1987 in Rehovot, Israel, is a pioneering researcher in virtual reality technology and artificial intelligence. With a Doctorate in Business Administration from EIASM and an MBA in Technological Entrepreneurship, Dr. Tubul- Lavy combines academic excellence with practical expertise. Holding diplomas in Photofinishing Engineering and Digital Media Engineering, Dr. Tubul-Lavy possesses a unique blend of technical knowledge and creative vision. He is a renowned authority in strategically implementing virtual and augmented reality technologies, helping organizations worldwide create immersive virtual worlds tailored for the business landscape. His specialization in integrating AI solutions with 3D technologies sets him apart in digital transformation. Dr. Tubul-Lavy has successfully led over 120 projects, deploying virtual world solutions internationally. His leadership extends to his role as Chairman of the Center of Excellence "Virtual Worlds & Metaverse" at the Israeli Chamber of Information Technology, where he drives innovation and excellence in the field. Dr. Tubul-Lavy is also the founder and entrepreneur behind the AI transcription and Hebrew analysis system Timlul.ai, a cutting-edge platform in Natural Language Processing. Dedicating his time to advancing research and developing groundbreaking solutions, Dr. Tubul-Lavy merges virtual worlds with AI to create transformative experiences. A speaker regularly presents at conferences and conducts workshops, sharing his insights and expertise with organizations looking to navigate the complexities of digital transformation. In 2016, Dr. Tubul-Lavy co-founded VR2GO Ltd, a company at the forefront of virtual reality implementation. In 2022, he joined the F- narrative venture as Head of R&D.

Beyond his professional achievements, Dr. Tubul- Lavy is a

family man, married to Rachel and father to Alona and Tamar. Hobbies: gamer, violinist.

For any question contact : zvitubul@gmail.com

JUNE 2024

ACKNOWLEDGMENTS

I want to express my deepest gratitude to several key individuals whose support has been invaluable throughout this journey. First and foremost, to my beloved wife, **Rachel**. Your unwavering support, patience, and encouragement have been the foundation for this work. You have given me the time and mental space needed to delve deeply into my research and write this e-book. For that and so much more, I am eternally grateful.

To my parents, Gila and Jacob, and my children, Alona and Tamar, your constant love and support are integral to my life. You have stood by me daily, providing the strength and motivation to pursue my dreams. This e-book is based on my doctoral thesis and reflects my extensive research in virtual worlds. It represents a significant part of my academic journey and professional endeavors. Additionally, another important aspect of my research is focused on artificial intelligence and its integration into the outcomes of my studies. This fascinating and rapidly evolving field will be addressed in a separate volume dedicated entirely to my work on AI. Thank you all for your support and belief in my work. This e-book is as much yours as it is mine.

Table Of Contents

Contents

ABOUT THE AUTHOR 3

ACKNOWLEDGMENTS 0

ABSTRACT...1

INDTRUDACTION 2

1. ....OVERVIEW
....4

1.1 WEB 1.0-2.0-3.0 LITERATURE REVIEW   1.1.1 WEB 1.0...5

1.1.2 WEB 2.0..6

1.1.3 WEB 3.0..8

1.2 VR LITERATURE REVIEW...11

1.3 METAVERSE LITERATURE REVIEW 16

1.4 VR METAVERSE VERSITES ARE THE NEW   WEBSITES
....18

2. MARKET GAPS AND THE PROBLEM 22

2.1.1 COVID-19 SOCIETY CHANGES 25

2.1.2 IMMERSION...29

2.1.3 COMPETITION AND SERIOUS GAMING 32

2.1.4 DESIGNING VIRTUAL REALITY   METAVERSE
BEST PRACTICE SUGGESTION..34

2.2 WHY DO BUSINESSES   AND ORGANIZATIONS NEED
TO TRANSFORM INTO VR METAVERSE.....................................43

2.2.1 WITHIN AN ORGANIZATION 45

2.2.2 OUTSIDE THE ORGANIZATION...53

2.3 THE PROBLEM AND PROCESS INHIBITORS 63

2.3.1 LIMITED ADOPTION 63

2.3.2 COMPLEXITY 64

2.3.3 SECURITY AND PRIVACY CONCERNS 64

2.3.4 LEGAL ISSUES 66

2.3.5 TIME-CONSUMING 67

2.3.6 NO PROTOCOLS...67

2.3.7 VERSITES COMPARING WEBSITES   AND SOCIAL
MEDIA 69

3. APPROACH AND SOLUTION 71

3.1 5 I'S MODEL 71

3.1.1 IMMERSION...73

3.1.2 INTERACTION..79

3.1.3 ILLUSTRATION...90

3.1.4 IMPACT 94

3.1.5 IMPLEMENTATION 99

3.2 THE SOLUTION- INVERSE BUILDER 105

3.2.1 INTRODUCTION 105

3.2.2 INVERSE NO-CODE VERSITES BUILDER 106

3.2.3 INVERSE BUILDER DESCRIPTION......................111

3.3 CASE STUDY RESULTS..117

3.3.1 BACKGROUND 118

3.3.2 SOLUTION- 5 I'S MODEL ANALYSIS 120

3.3.3 THE ITALIAN CASE-RESULTS   AND CONCLUSION
....130

4. SUMMARY..133

4.1 SUMMARY AND CONCLUSION 133

4.2 LIMITATION...135

4.3 SUGGESTIONS FOR FURTHER   RESEARCH 137

4.4 APPLAY ARTIFICIAL INTELLIFENCE IN   FURTHER
RESEARCH..139

5. REFERENCES 141

ABSTRACT

Virtual worlds have existed for about thirty years. In recent years, supporting technologies and revolutionary concepts have changed how users consume virtual worlds and are now involved in the Internet revolution. The internet revolution of the virtual worlds will force businesses to get to know the new tools and make an effective transformation to the virtual worlds and maximize their business potential.

Technological challenges and the lack of familiarity with the recently developing language cause failure in the transformation process. In this thesis, I created two tools for businesses to succeed in the process and increase their chances of success. The first tool offers the "5 I's model", which examines five main parameters for analysis before implementing a transformation process into virtual worlds. The second tool provides low-budget businesses with simple software based on an intuitive drag-and- drop method to build virtual worlds based on the "5 i's model." I developed the tools by analyzing over 120 projects implementing virtual worlds and virtual reality technologies in various segments during 2016-2023. To offer the best practice for creating virtual worlds, the indicators that affect the user experience were examined. Also, all the projects were divided into categories to explain why businesses use virtual worlds.

Finally, a case study describes a successful implementation of the model in practice and invites firms to use the transformation model. With the development of technology, it will be necessary to make adjustments to the model, and therefore, the model is open to adjustments through further research.

INTRUDACTION

Life is a sequence of images processed in the human mind. The memories of humans are engraved on digital media and create an unimaginable amount of information.

Humans' abilities to create information have evolved with the development of technology and the available media. According to Domo (Sleeps, 2021), ordinary people generate 1.7 MB every second. The main motive for generating so much information is the need for communication and socializing. Hence, humanity constantly strives to improve communication methods through digital media devices that always arouse curiosity. Historically, humans have been exposed to new media such as radio, television, and the internet. Each of the latter causes disruption and brings opportunities as well as challenges. Digital transformation is the ability of organizations to change their approach to how the organization is managed and keep it active and alive alongside new technologies. Organizations that do not adopt innovation and do not undertake to go through digital transformation processes impose a death sentence on themselves sooner or later.

Due to the importance of the topic of digital transformation to the survival of organizations, I saw fit to analyze and draw conclusions from over 120 digital transformation projects. According to the thesis, organizations must understand the criteria to consider when implementing the virtual worlds as a part of this process. The objectives of the thesis are:

1. Produce a detailed model of the five essential parameters for applying digital transformation to the virtual worlds.

2. Bring an easy-to-use Drag & Drop software to the world based on the five parameters and make the virtual worlds accessible to

businesses.

The first part proposed a model called the 5 i's (iiiii) that will detail Immersion, Interaction, Illustration, Impact, and Implementation. Understanding the criteria and early planning of the transformation process will help organizations successfully navigate the complex process into the metaverse world. I open the model to the world and anticipate that it will expand with technological improvement and, even in certain parts, will be reduced due to the setting of standards in the field that will eliminate the decision-making process from the leaders of the processes in the organizations.

The second part of the thesis will deal with creating a no-code platform to serve companies that want to perform the digital transformation process in an accessible and easy way without coding. The system includes implementing most parameters proposed in the 5-i's model. Also, the software aims to make it easier for small and medium-sized businesses for whom the digital transformation process is more complicated and usually requires a lot of resources. Using the platform will save enterprises human resources, money, and development time, as well as months of software requirements documents and understanding of the language and interaction of the media. With those thesis's outcomes, businesses can easily adopt a virtual world presence and benefit from the virtual world's value

1. OVERVIEW

This section provides a comprehensive review of the evolution of the internet from Web.

1.0 to Web 3.0, as well as a review of virtual reality (VR), the metaverse, and the combination of both in the VR metaverse. The Web 1.0 to Web 3.0 literature review highlights the major technological advancements and changes in internet usage patterns over the years. The virtual reality literature review examines the development and applications of VR technology, including its use in various fields. The metaverse literature review the concept of a shared virtual space that is accessed by users through the internet and its potential impact on society. Finally, the VR metaverse literature review explores the combination of VR and the metaverse, discussing the potential of creating immersive virtual environments experiences.

Today, there is still no unequivocal and agreed definition of WEB 3.0. There is debate in the industry and disagreements about what is included under this new disruptive term. Organizations are wondering how they should prepare for the day when WEB 3.0 will become the standard as WEB 2.0 did, from 2004 until today. To answer this question and predict the challenges that organizations will face, we will briefly go back to the history of the Internet, starting with WEB 1.0, and present the changes in perception and supporting technologies.

I will present my opinion and subjective definition of the user's status in the various generations to convey the message of change in users, threats, and opportunities in organizations.

1.1 WEB 1.0-2.0-3.0 LITERATURE REVIEW

1.1.1 WEB 1.0

Beginning in 1991, at the beginning of the Internet, web pages and various sites included information pages only, "read-only" (Cormode & Krishnamurthy, 2008). There were no user login detection systems or options for creating content by them, like blogs or talkbacks, nor data collection (as known today). Internet advertisements have yet to generate economic margins. It can be said with a broad and superficial look that the Internet, in its first version, was a pile of information presented to the user. The internet created a significant disruption, and businesses required an internet presence. But it is important to note that no complex technologies supported Web 1.0 (Breeding, 2006).

The static state of the pages created an encyclopedia-like representation that can be browsed indefinitely and viewed on the same pages with the same content. The user was ineffective. While two users watched the same link, they saw the same thing so that we could call the users "consumers." The role of the user was to consume the content and nothing more. Over the years, web tools such as Java, Flash, and HTML developed and significantly changed pages and how they are consumed.

It is not possible to indicate the exact date when the change occurred. Still, it is possible to indicate a sequence of changes that allowed the early adopters to implement the changes until they entered the mainstream. Those changes are also related to the pace of emergence and use of end equipment, such as computers, smartphones, and tablets, a topic we will leave to another article.

1.1.2 WEB 2.0

Around 2004, there was a significant change in the role of the consumer. If, until now, the information moved one way, from the site to the user, now the information movement has become two-way. Organizations have begun to collect data on the consumer. The transition to a two-way connection caused a revolution, which initially did not seem disruptive. The first to read the map marched forward. Significant giant corporations were born in this revolution in various areas, including social networks, tourism companies, search engines, rating systems, virtual malls, advertising and marketing, and virtually all areas of life . At that time, companies collected user data and presented custom content (personalization) to make a profit. Moreover, a significant step in data collection has created a secondary market (no less profitable)

of trading in customer information in favor of targeted advertising. This move made the consumer the product. Data collection also caused significant disruption to the end users. Users had to give up (with approval or not) their privacy since information collected about them is not only held by the organization that manages it. The users' data goes on and trades. Every consumer is known and familiar with the information collection systems, down to the most individual level - if he has a family, what vehicle he is driving in, and up to the ability to predict issues the consumer did not know about himself. For example, a married couple living in the same household (same IP for that matter, or the same GPS coordinates) with a couple of children. Suppose the husband seeks to surprise his wife and children and adopt a dog. A search on the parent network conducts searches on dog types, adoption sites, treatment and breeding methods, preferred foods, and even tips for training and playing with children. The moment the generator collects the data, the woman pops up advertisements and various ads to purchase dog accessories, such as bowls designed to her liking and "accidentally" straps offered in her three favorite colors. The consumer is the one who has given up privacy for content customization, which over time has become an industry standard, as the consumer had no choice but to share the information about him if he wanted to continue using the internet services. The two-way information model means that the same link to a particular site is processed for different versions depending on the viewer, so we would not have to go through the same experience as an anonymous entity. This is how the Facebook feed looks different and so are the prices of flights on the same website, which differ from person to person.

1.1.3 WEB 3.0

The interesting question is, when will Web 3.0 arrive, and what will be the difference in the user's status? All readers of these lines have experienced Web 2.0 in full force and want to know if the state of information storage and privacy is about to change. This is where new supporting technologies (Rudman & Bruwer, 2016) and another change of perception come into play. I will detail innovative technologies like blockchain, artificial intelligence, and more in other articles.

I am constantly unequivocally careful, as it is not yet clear what a day will bring in terms of technology, so it is said that the consumer will have some control over the content, with a significant emphasis on knowing that this control is limited to the time of publication. If in Web 2.0 we emphasized that the user is the product and the corporations are the content owners, in Web 3.0 the user becomes the content owner and is responsible for his data. Example: If we uploaded a post with a photo or video attached to Web 3.0, we do own the content, but the posts and attachments to it are now duplicated in the blockchain network and not registered on just one specific site on a particular server farm where the information is stored. Although blockchain technology has a high level of security, the technology also has some disadvantages (Golosova & Romanovs, 2018). We notice that some main risks, such as offensive, insulting, inappropriate, or illegal information, will emerge under the guise of freedom of expression without censorship of collaborative platforms. Because content owners are consumers, it will be difficult up to Impossible to cancel its publication.

We will discuss a few more differences. Following the last example, Web 2.0 is defined as customized and dynamic content, while Web 3.0 has not yet defined the essence of the content and how the information flows. Some assumptions of unclear definitions, such as Rudman & Bruwer (2016) suggested that machines will understand information. I can't refute it, but I can suggest that the definition is more complex than suggested. This question will accompany us with uncertainty soon, and the picture will become clear by the time Web 3.0 becomes common.

The key point in Web 2.0 was tagging users and optimizing the content for them and thus affecting their purchase decisions (Kaulina & Kaulins, 2018), while in Web 3.0 the focus shifts to the user, and its empowerment is central and based on high-level trust, privacy, and security. While in Web 2.0 the focus was on building communities and treating the community as a body that could be targeted or used, for example, in its purchasing power, in Web 3.0 the focus is on the individual user and his power to make decisions and changes as an individual. The types of applications in Web 2.0 were closed applications, while Web 3.0 supports blockchain, artificial intelligence-driven, and machine-learning applications (Alabduwahhab,2018). Moreover, most importantly - the user can be anonymous in his identity and perform all the desired actions.

Implementing and using a blockchain encourages information sharing but maintains privacy. The true identity of the user in daily life does not require disclosure. The user's virtual identity (can be a representative number) can be recognized as active while everyone is watching the moves and actions he performs on the network, including the banking activity if his wallet number is exposed. In the Web 3.0 era, we anticipate that imaginary or alternative virtual environments will be created, allowing individuals to produce an alternative activity to the real world.

Some will go so far as to say that the user is fed up with huge octopus corporations with bureaucracy and tremendous influence on the user, and this is the opportunity to reshape the world. Ambitious? Time will tell.

Having briefly reviewed the development of Web 3.0, I will present several points that characterize the disruption and have a potential impact on business organizations.

1. Creation of oligopoly markets bypassing corporations.
2. Blurring the boundaries of the real and virtual world.
3. Return of ownership of the information to the consumer.
4. Secure data sharing between entities.
5. Immunity from governmental decisions (making moves without the ability to monitor government).
6. Organizational immunity due to shortening the supply chain.

Each of these points invites a separate article on the future impact and how to build the organizations and centers of power in the economy.

1.2 VR LITERATURE REVIEW

Virtual reality is not a new concept. It has been around for decades, with the first patent filed in 1968. The technology has evolved from bulky, expensive, and low-quality to today's more affordable, lightweight, and high-quality headsets.

The beginning of the history of virtual reality is in the era of photography and the change of perception from two-dimensional to three-dimensional. Back in time to 1841, in stereoscopic photography (Junevičius,2022) - people could view two images with an overlap of about 30% and turn them into one three-dimensional image. This is the first time we saw an upgrade of two-dimensional art to turn it into virtual reality. The feeling of three-dimensionality allows people to watch through a device with two lenses that disconnect them from the environment and allow them to watch in a three-dimensional environment. In those years, unlike today, many people were not accessible to transportation and could not visit distant places. So the genre of "traveling the world" was a best-seller in those days, and many people would sell series of images to view with binoculars (Leotta & Ross, 2018). About a hundred years later, the devices were widespread worldwide, and entire encyclopedias were sold for educational purposes, such as the human body in medicine. In those days, there was a desire to abandon the glasses and watch 3D without an intermediary. Many attempts have been made, including viewing a picture on a wall and looking left and right to see a different picture. However, the viewer was exposed to the environment, and viewing a picture on a wall failed to signal the experience of personal glasses. In the decade that began in 1960, the first device that interpreted Virtual Reality as a sensory experience that is not only visual came to the market. At that time, the device was called Sensorama. It included 3D viewing, the possibility for the viewer to move his head left and right, sound from several directions, and high-pressure air activated at specific points during the projected film (García-Pereira et-al., 2020). Those times saw NASA's first attempts to use the technology to simulate an environment with a space shuttle. When in 1965, HMD (Helmet Mounted Display) was introduced for the first time by Ivan Sutherland. Later the abbreviation HMD became known as Head Mounted Display. (SUTHERLAND 2021).

His research in those days was groundbreaking, and IVAN is considered one of the most important fathers in the successful journey of virtual reality technology. In his writings, he describes the ultimate helmet that, even then (1965) included head movement sensors and synchronization between the display and the user's viewing angle. Research topics that in those days were science fiction.

In the 80s, we will mention a key figure, Professor Randy Pausch. Pausch specializes in human-machine communication and has a decade-long education history and has worked in companies such as XEROX, ADOBE, and WALT DISNEY. At this crucial point in time, Pausch's contribution is the ability to create interactive multiplayer virtual environments. Which so far has been said to have used virtual reality technology for a single player.

In 1991 we saw an arcade machine designed for the entertainment market for the first time. The device included a low-quality helmet with no color saturation and a limited number of costly games. The device was used by the consumer sitting down. VIRTUAL BOY is the name of the first virtual reality HMD that came to the market for the Nintendo company a few years after the publication of the SEGA company. The product failed due to its high price, the computer required to run it, the graphics with two colors, and the minimal number of games released, which are four optional games. The global company SEGA later produced a home console with virtual reality glasses, which was, for many years, a marketing move and nothing more than that because the promised glasses were never released (Liao et-al, 2020).

The virtual reality market in those days intended to revolutionize the way we consume content and the way we operate in the world. A revolution that, in retrospect, was ahead of its time. The VR headsets were expensive and not very user-friendly. They also required much space to use them, which made them impractical for most people. The graphics were also not good enough to make it an enjoyable experience for most people. After these attempts to raise virtual reality awareness and turn it into a breakthrough technology - the market cooled, and there was a pause of about two decades until the second attempt came. In 2009, Palmer Lucky began the vision of creating VR glasses accessible to the general public. Lucky created the initial prototype from lenses of reasonable quality with a wide angle of view not never before seen in virtual reality glasses. The correction for the distortion of the lenses was done through software and not the quality of the glass, and thus they were able to achieve a relatively light and small helmet for home use. Lucky worked on the project for three years in the garage of his parent's house, and he was 16 years old at the time. At the launch of a crowdfunding project on Kickstarter, Lucky won the support of central and well-known figures in the gaming world who declared that they believed in Lucky and called to back the project (Harley, 2020). The project succeeded far beyond expectations, and while Lucky asked for $250,000, he managed to raise $2.5 million. At the end of 2014, OCULUS (the name of Lucky's virtual reality glasses) was purchased by Facebook. Until that year, Lucky and VALVE company worked in cooperation. Since Facebook acquired OCULUS, their paths diverged, and each company worked on a different tracking system and based the HMD on different operating systems. In 2016, a turning point occurred when three major companies launched virtual reality glasses for the home consumer.

Facebook launched the Oculus Rift, PlayStation launched their first virtual reality helmet, and HTC, in collaboration with VALVE, launched VIVE, which initially undoubtedly brought the highest quality to the market with the best tracking system. In those days, VIVE could allow the user a whole experience of walking in free space with the help of the tracking system, compared to the other helmets of the same year that only allowed playing while sitting. In 2018, Oculus Rift narrowed the gap with VIVE when they significantly improved the content offering and the ability to compare tracking capabilities and allow playing not only while sitting. It should be noted that in those days, Microsoft made a combined move with large companies in the market that included ACER, HP, DELL, and many more and launched a helmet with a different tracking called INSIDE OUT without external sensors, supposedly a significant innovation. However, the tracking was not successful, and the helmet quality was not able to compete with VIVE and OCULUS, so it failed. Also, in the same year (2018), the second and most professional version of VIVE was launched, which was aimed at the business market. The helmet was indeed more expensive but of significantly higher quality, more professional with elements such as built-in headphones, improved internal microphone, and of course, the resolution. At the end of 2018, several changes in the market again devoured the cards. OCULUS came out with a new version called QUEST, which killed their previous product that came out at the same time called OCULUS RIFT S. The QUEST did not require a connection to a computer and worked independently, and was preferred over its brother RIFT S. In the same year, VALVE dissolved the partnership with VIVE. It turned to the development and launch of a high- quality helmet with a high price tag called VALVE INDEX, which maintained a high position thanks to the quality of the display, the refresh rate speed, and the special remotes that recognized the number of fingers holding the remote and enabled a different and precise style of games. This year there was a breakthrough and a significant increase in the virtual reality market when millions of glasses units were sold, stocks were running out in warehouses, and the market remained high in demand. We note that support for best-seller games is one of the strongest engines for purchasing helmets.

The OCULUS QUEST was strengthened by support for the most addictive and popular game in those days, BEAT SABER, which garnered millions of sales. Moreover, HTC VIVE supported the highest quality game at the graphical level that every VR player knows, aka HALF LIFE ALYX. The race to create the best helmet is not yet complete. Every year there are big announcements and attempts to fill a void in additional markets, both in the professional and low-cost markets.

Virtual reality is still in its infancy, but it has been making strides in recent years. With better hardware and software that are more affordable, there is no doubt that VR will continue to grow and become even more immersive for users.

1.3 METAVERSE LITERATURE REVIEW

Metaverse is a combination of words - META, which means beyond understanding or the conscious, and VERSE, an abbreviation of the word Universe. The term first appeared in Neil Stevenson's "Snow Crash" book in 1992. It is common to refer to the word metaverse as a three-dimensional virtual world, on the scale of the real world (or beyond), where the user has a representative character (avatar) and an emotional and sentimental affinity for the world. Interacting with other users is a crucial element that can be performed on any digital device, such as a computer, console, smartphone, or virtual reality glasses.

Whether users believe in metaverse or not, the world is moving towards it in giant strides. GTC conference (by NVIDIA) September 2022, all the most important statements about the future of technology are concentrated in this conference. Rev Lebaredian, VP of Omniverse & Simulation Technology, said in his lecture - "The Metaverse is an extension of the Internet as we know it. It is the evolution of the Internet"... "We are going to create a new language, where we will take the ideas in our heads and build immersive worlds around us." (Shale, 2022). There are disagreements about exactly what the metaverse is, its effects, and whether it is already here or still in the development stages. What is certain is that the metaverse has entered the general public's consciousness in recent years. As proof of this, we can see an increasing number of searches for the phrase METAVERSE on Google and YouTube, publications of professional academic magazines focused on METAVERSE, and article publications (Narin, 2021).

One of the definitions of the Metaverse describes the post-realistic world, a multiplayer virtual environment combining senses and interactions. The Metaverse is the environment that connects the

technology, the principles of the new world, the challenges that the world brings with it, and the capabilities that invite the user to experiment (Mystakidis, 2022). Part of the review will focus on what the Metaverse is not.

Metaverse is not new and has been with us for several decades. Any multiplayer computer game with the interaction between the participants meets the definition. Metaverse is not a technology in itself. It is the space where the technologies meet and serve as a platform to make them accessible to the user. Metaverse is not just a computer game, although it contains one of the platform's most essential elements, gamification. Moreover, another claim is that the metaverse belongs not to one body or corporation but to the whole. Millions of metaverses will arise as internet sites exist.

Matthew Ball (2022) describes in his book the Metaverse as a world that synchronously exists in real-time, in three dimensions. It allows communication between an unlimited number of users when everyone feels the sense of presence in the world that data exists and continues to be created.

1.4 VR METAVERSE VERSITES ARE THE NEW WEBSITES

We should not confuse the terms "virtual reality" (VR) with "metaverse" since the metaverse can exist without VR, and not all VR experiences are metaverse. The confusion was created due to META's statement (formerly Facebook), which offered a virtual world that uses virtual reality glasses only. At the same time, there is likely a close interface between the virtual worlds and virtual reality technology. Most technology giants (including Meta, Nvidia, Google, and Apple) are devoting resources to the field, and we expect a real revolution in the coming years. It will not be possible to ignore or not be part of the revolution. Even the most skeptical, those who have argued that online shopping will not be popular, agree that there will be a digital transformation of most markets and organizations in the next decade.

VR metaverse is already used today to streamline processes and improve profitability. A uniform methodology for digital transformation and entry into the metaverse still needs to be uniform. This requires a specific characterization for each organization since the application in the field varies between the different industries. The metaverse uses gamification, so corporations can be seen acquiring game studios. For example, Microsoft acquired Blizzard Entertainment for about $ 70 billion (still under regulation examination right for Jan 2023). These processes signal that in the not-too-distant future, we will experience blurring between the virtual world and the real world so that the two-dimensional language of websites will be replaced by an experience of using three-dimensional worlds, with virtual representations, connections, products, environments, and stores for work in virtual offices. I call this 3D website- Versite as a term that describes Virtual Site. A website refers to the textual language and offers a place on the Internet to display content

(Brügger, 2009). The term website theoretically should have changed long ago since websites are based on much more than textual language. The visual language took center stage with the development of the web, but the name remained as it was. There is room to propose a new name to characterize the virtual worlds. The term I propose refers to the VERSITES that will replace the websites with an emphasis on the language and the user interface. The environments of the virtual worlds speak an interactive three-dimensional language. The interaction and use of a three-dimensional interface are entirely different from the use of websites. Therefore, consideration must be given to changing the name that indicates the product. VERSITES are intended to mark on the timeline in history a fundamental change in how consumers consume information online. The essential change should reach every website owner who must carry out a digital transformation and adopt the new language to reach the target audience. Those who do not do this will realize too late that they will lose customers who will not return. These days remind those skeptics in the 2000s who despised websites and continued to appear in indexes and printed business cards.

In the world of medicine - several applications that already exist in the market include training surgeons in a virtual environment, a forgiving environment for mistakes, and encouraging learning and experience. Another application is meetings between doctors or between doctors and patients in a virtual environment without creating contact, which can bridge distance gaps.

In the world of tourism - a virtual visit to interesting cities expands the clientele even to populations that do not travel and vacation due to medical restrictions, age restrictions, or socioeconomic status. Now an opportunity arises to allow, at a very low cost, a visit anywhere in the world by using virtual reality and creating a metaverse for shared tours with friends and family. For example, a unique Israeli project called Better Life VR allows seniors to travel the world and watch the performing arts, meet relatives and even witness occupations and hobbies that their bodies can no longer perform and thus restore their joy of life and dispel loneliness.

The worlds of education - successful applications for teacher training and simulations eliminate expensive simulations with the help of players and instructors since all the players are virtual and respond using artificial intelligence. This training can save space resources as there is no need to create learning environments. Everything is digital, and users can enter the virtual world from anywhere, whether it is from home or work.

Worlds of the automotive industry - a significant application in the field of car design proved even more effective in 2019 when some designers in different places met in a virtual world and performed a week task that would take them about a month in the real world. Another application that led to a 30% increase in car sales in Audi showrooms - a customer goes into their metaverse and designs the car for himself as he would like - paint, upholstery, add or subtract elements and order a car tailored for him. The company makes an additional profit as it is unnecessary to bring many vehicles with different finish levels to the showrooms.

The worlds of advertising and marketing - Many brands (such as Gucci, Samsung, Hyundai, Nike, Disney, and more) have already opened a specialty store in the metaverse, allowing customers to experience a three-dimensional experience.

Worlds of Law Enforcement Training - The EU has significantly increased the number of grants for cross-country training projects in the virtual worlds. Thus, several projects have been carried out to train wardens, judges, and police officers in different courses, saving millions of dollars by saving human resources for training outside the country.

In addition, millions of dollars have been saved in creating virtual training environments, Accessories in space, etc. The situation can be restored to its original state with the click of a button.

2. MARKET GAPS AND THE PROBLEM

In this section, we will analyze the digital era gap and explore how virtual reality can potentially overcome these gaps. We will examine the limitations and shortcomings of current digital technologies and identify areas where VR can offer a more immersive and engaging experience.We will examine the challenges organizations face in designing and implementing VR metaverse environments that meet the needs of their users. We will explore factors such as user adoption, cost, and technical feasibility that impact the successful implementation of VR metaverse environments. Next, we will define the market problem when applying digital transformation to the VR metaverse.Finally, we will discuss how to build best practices for designing a VR metaverse environment. This includes exploring fundamental design principles and considerations like user experience, accessibility, and scalability. We will examine how VR technology can be leveraged to create engaging, immersive experiences that meet users' needs. We will also explore the role of collaboration and co-creation in designing VR metaverse environments that reflect users' diverse needs and preferences.

2.1 VR METAVERSE-GAPS OVERVIEW AND SUGGESTIONS FOR BEST PRACTICE DESIGNING A VR METAVERSE ENVIRONMENT

Although Virtual Reality (VR) started being used in the 80s, in the last decade, the number of users sharply increased due to the development of more friendly and not-for- expert devices, the favorable market, and the advent of events such as the COVID-19 outbreak. Especially in specific sectors such as education or the labor market, the pandemic has brought a technological revolution that will likely last beyond COVID-19.

The "Metaverse" buzzword appeared in October 2021 when Facebook decided to rebrand and change the company name to Meta as a referral to METAVERSE vision.

The change causes colossal disruption and forecasts the change in the social interaction on the web (Kraus at-al, 2022).

Despite the statement at the end of 2021, the metaverse has existed for about 30 years. The virtual worlds claim to be a digital replica of the real world, giving the user a "realistic experience." However, a realistic experience can be characterized by many factors ranging from the graphic level to intuitive interaction that simulates a person's natural action. Moreover, to create the feeling of a realistic experience, we must start with the roots that build the VR metaverse and refine the factors that can help us maintain the ultimate user experience.

Before the architectural stage, the first step in developing VR metaverse is to examine failures and successes from various digital experiments relating to areas tangent to training, learning, and interactions in the digital space. This examination is for an internal evaluation of the medium's advantages in the architectural mapping phase. It emphasizes features that can be a significant advantage for realizing the vision, improving, and streamlining the building process using virtual reality technology.

2.1.1 COVID-19 SOCIETY CHANGES

To define the necessary features for VR metaverse development, one must examine the limitations and gaps in digital interactions and the implications of the COVID-19 pandemic on our relationship as humanity.

Italy, for example, is among the countries that have experienced the most severe outbreak and spread of the pandemic. Italy was among the first to make intervention moves as restricted movement between districts or out of the country. The actions' impact reduced residents' activity by an average of 50%. Another restriction imposed is remote work, meaning that the state encouraged workplaces to operate the workforce remotely and to avoid meetings (Pepe et al., 2020).

In the field of conferences, a significant impact was recorded when all conferences and meetings were stopped in one moment. The conferences also generated traffic for people on flights and tourism. They developed human capital in interpersonal meetings in which the people shared knowledge and listened to lectures by authorities in their field. Thousands of canceled conferences directly affected the organizations participating in these events. Now, a window of opportunity for digital activity has opened, and many players have entered the market to provide the ideal digital conference. The EDBT / ICDT conference that was supposed to occur in Copenhagen was canceled three weeks before it took place with the start of the COVID-19 pandemic. The event organizers decided to move the conference online for the first time. They built the conference with a vision of "trying to preserve as much of the real-life experience as possible" (Bonifati et-al., 2020).

The organizers made several choices to create an event that ostensibly supported the vision. Shortening the posters' display

time makes it easier for the viewer from home. They were moving the conference synchronously with the help of several programs, including ZOOM for viewing and using SLACK for discussion. To reduce the possibility of technical malfunctions at broadcasting, all talks were pre-recorded and broadcast at a fixed time, the questions answered before and after the broadcast. The coffee breaks between the sessions were shortened to 15 minutes max to shorten the days. The poster display is grouped into a chain of video presentations without interaction.

Hosting and broadcasting the presentations based on the technical equipment in the exhibitor's possession relied on the exhibitor's internet connection stability. Most decisions contradict a 'life experience' vision, from separating the presenter from the viewers to shortening the coffee breaks intended for networking as a central part of the event (Stokel-Walker, 2020).

According to the questionnaires collected after the conference, the responses spoke for themselves; 80 out of 111 respondents stated that they 'agree' and 'strongly agree' with the statement: 'Did the conference need more social interaction?' In addition to the further questions, most of the presenters felt uncomfortable with the technology of facing a camera. They preferred to record the lectures in advance, which was against the participants' will.

A qualitative study examined the quality of communication between an interviewer and an interviewee through a video call in messaging software versus a face-to-face meeting (Gray, Wong-Wylie, Rempel & Cook, 2020). The test was done on ZOOM software (Zoom video communications INC.) Nevertheless, it also applies to similar messaging software such as Skype, Google Meet, etc. The study examines the relationship quality in a video call when this is not possible face-to-face. The most notable advantage is the savings in travel time and the cost of flights for an interview or meeting and security in interviewing in the event of unforeseen

external events such as storms or road delays. However, we are here to examine the researchers' recommendations and learn about the gaps to see the possibility of assimilating the ultimate solution in a virtual reality metaverse environment. Essential points of recommendation focused, among other things, on technical issues such as a preliminary examination of the technology before the meeting and providing technical information about technical operations such as selecting sound sources configured in the computer settings. In addition, a backup plan is essential in case of technological failure, checking for a stable internet connection of the participating parties or eliminating connection interruptions like GSM calls. Additional recommendations are distraction prevention that may result from each party in its own private space full of daily distractions. With all the recommendations, one can think of adding elements of artificial intelligence to facilitate the automatic transcription process.

The main disadvantage the researchers pointed out is the interviewee's physical space and the interviewers' differences. As a result, it is difficult for the interviewer to respond to the interviewee's body movements and emotional cues. There is also a problem of uncontrollable distractions due to the interviewee choosing the space he is being interviewed. It is difficult to avoid distractions in his private environment instead of a face-to-face encounter in a shared physical space.

Looking at the recent past and the beginning of social sharing, we can get information from a study that examined sharing cross-border academic knowledge. The study finds several vital characteristics that elevate the quality of the experience and learning, including social learning consolidation, higher learning abilities in a support group, and knowledge sharing -also learning strategies to overcome language gaps between countries (Correia, Baran & Yusop, 2007).

In another article, out of the 126 respondents, half completed high school, and half of them, undergraduate students, reported 78.6% for higher effectiveness in face-to-face studies and the vital presence of a learning guide (Adnan & Anwar, 2020).

Traditional education is also deeply rooted in academic education systems, where one can see the opposition of lecturers to adopting new technologies. They claim to have turned them from frontal presenters accustomed to direct interaction and visual communication into educational technology experts whose role is reduced (Lassoued et-al., 2020). This claim lowers the motivation in the learning process on the part of the educator and deprives the students of proper education. Another obstacle stems from the inability to evaluate students' assignments in the digital environment, the difficulty in discovering the strengths and weaknesses of each student, and proper pedagogical treatment. The students also expressed low motivation for distance learning due to the need for more space for direct interaction. More and more obstacles are exposed in information security and privacy; these directly affect the exams' results and the participants' identity. This gap can easily change the examinee's identity and even cheat during the exam. Last but not least, the difficulty of providing technology in every home in a space detached from the daily troubles of the home makes the learning process difficult.

In adopting new technology, we know there is a significant barrier in training the staff who will be the trainers on the field. However, it is an opportunity to harness the veteran teams for significant change. With supportive and skilled staff, adopting and implementing the technology will be easier, as seen in similar areas such as telemedicine (Smith et-al., 2020).

2.1.2 IMMERSION

While virtual reality has existed for about five decades, competition for user emotions has escalated recently. Influencing the user's emotions is part of a necessary process in the virtual reality metaverse that constructs the language of the medium. Immersion is based on a user's perceptual change during the experience that makes him doubt his presence in an imaginary world and gives him the feeling that he is indeed experiencing real emotions and a situation. To achieve such a state of mind, many methods are required to develop the experience; the more the latter increase, the greater the sense of immersion.

Total immersion is only sometimes required to get the desired result, and the tools to achieve the goal must be carefully examined (Bowman & McMahan, 2007). Sometimes a minor use of the new language's tools for the virtual reality metaverse is sufficient. In other cases, excessive assimilation tools can cause extreme and ineffective sensory stimulation and impair the experience.

Even before the portable and lightweight virtual reality devices we know today, we witnessed many studies are done about two decades ago that examined the key factors that affect the quality of immersion. The main findings show the user's excitement from experience, comfort in the virtual environment, and sound and image quality. (Riva et-al., 1998).

These factors guide how to think when developing a metaverse environment that directs the development process to touch the user's emotions and put him at the center. This is how the language of virtual reality is constructed, in contrast to the cinematic language, where there is an emphasis on leading the viewer and creating interest in him to remain watching the plot. In VR metaverse, a change of direction requires thought around the viewer and not in front of him. Some unique virtual reality tools that build a sense of immersion include presence and embodiment body ownership, competition, and Serious gaming. Applied tools that cannot be produced in any other media.

Therefore, there is also a significant gap in the terminology when in the cinema or similar media, we say "the viewer."

In contrast, we say "the user" in virtual reality since he uses the media actively and does not stare at the screen passively. The tools' description helps to understand the basis for creating an immersive shared location, which will be described in the next section of the article. A deep understanding of these tools is complex and requires extensive knowledge of virtual space creation. However, the details of the sub-tools demonstrated in this article will be more accessible.

Presence is a key tool for achieving immersion. The sense of presence is a behavioral correlation between a person in a computer-generated environment and his reactions as if in a real-world (Sanchez-Vives & Slater, 2005). This feeling is a sensory delusion in which the presence moves to another dimension other than the reality in which we live. Some of the following tools can be given up or used little, but this tool is the basis for creating an immersive experience.

The following tool helps to connect the user with his virtual avatar emotionally and physically way so that the user feels ownership and connection to the virtual body at the biological level. The embodiment experience can be so powerful that the user can create an identity exchange. Kilteni, Groten, & Slater (2012) propose a more in-depth analysis of three sub-components that make up the sense of embodiment. In their paper, they present some studies to substantiate this claim and extensive suggestions for future experiments to improve virtual reality applications and virtual worlds in general.

Body ownership can be considered an extension of the previous section, in which identification with the new body takes place. This type of identification was examined concerning physical responses to virtual events. It was found that users who experience identification with their virtual body respond rationally to events that threaten the virtual body. A high level of body ownership strengthens the immersion level by that it causes the user to respond to virtual events as if they were real. The level of identification can be raised or lowered according to content in the virtual world using tools available to content developers, as can be found in the article by Gonzalez-Franco et al. (2010), the manipulation of body reflection synchronously or asynchronously that affected the level of identification of users with the virtual body and the avoidance of encountering a digital image of a fan.

2.1.3 COMPETITION AND SERIOUS GAMING

Competitiveness is a crucial tool for developing games in general and not necessarily in the context of virtual reality. In every game nowadays, one can find an element of competition, whether between humans and machines or between humans and humans. Competitiveness is one of the engines of enjoyment in the game and creates interest in the user and allows him to set goals that need to be reached to win. Competitiveness is part of human nature and is inherent in most games we are familiar with.

The serious game indicates the use of gamification to convey educational messages or for training purposes that are a competitive element aimed at training for learning and improvement and are not included in the entertainment field for the private user. The term gamification can often be found in institutions, organizations, commercial companies, and governments.

A study examining the effectiveness of competitiveness and collaboration between virtual reality users found that game participants who created collaborations shared more knowledge than teams competing. Nevertheless, the players competing with each other in teams were more curious and explored more virtual space. Also, competitive participants retained interest and focus time significantly concerning players who did not compete and engaged solely in cooperation. In addition, whether competing or collaborating, active players within a team tend to remember more visual things in the environment (Liang et al., 2019). Connecting players in a virtual environment and adding elements of competitiveness can be more significant emotional stimulation than the human-machine competition (Lim & Reeves, 2010). Also, players have a higher sense of presence when playing against real people's avatars and not a machine.

2.1.4 DESIGNING VIRTUAL REALITY METAVERSE BEST PRACTICE SUGGESTION

The comprehensive literature review conducted before the commencement of work presented a long list of discrepancies discovered in similar products. To learn and draw lessons from similar products, I decided to examine each gap and offer a technological, design, or practical solution to get the most out of the process and provide a high-value product. It is appropriate to share the knowledge so that developers worldwide can produce experiences at a higher level and even share the knowledge further and give value from continuous improvement.

2.1.4.1 LOCATION GAPS AND TRAFFIC RESTRICTIONS

Regarding location gaps in the COVID-19 epidemic, flight and travel times consume much time for trainers and trainees (or any other two or more people). While the flight is not an option, other types of meetings are needed. My development team and I rewrote the code built before the pandemic started (as a single-player) and changed it to multiplayer so that the need to fly or travel to perform interaction in meetings is not required anymore. Also, the requirement of remote work did not allow people to get to the workplace where the equipment usually exists; cross-platform support, either PC or VR headset, allowed us to perform the activity from anywhere in the world with a basic internet connection. While other media bridges time gaps, virtual reality allows for bridging space gaps and meeting in a shared space.

2.1.4.2 TECHNICAL MALFUNCTION

In all communication devices and software, we can find glitches caused by software or customers' equipment. One way or another, there will always be faults, and it is necessary to understand where the weak points are and create simple solutions for them. On the software side, for quality assurance (QA) reasons, I made connections from several different countries to the multiplayer system I developed with my team. As well as on different bandwidths to check the stability of the software. I sampled a variety of connection qualities. Since the host computer connection was critical to the stability of the other participants, I saw fit to switch to cloud technology. The server is hosted in a GCP (GOOGLE CLOUD PLATFORM) environment and is located in Central Europe with backups in different regions. The cloud environment can be moved or replicated to various centers worldwide to create an optimal participant connection environment. This method avoids the need for a quality connection on the client's side. The only requirement is a good WIFI connection. Still, my recommendation is to work on a LAN connection. The lowest internet connection I used was a 1.5MB LAN speed for an exhibition in Doha in Qatar. At the same time, participants were both local and international, and the hosting server was in Europe. It is important to note that from a technical point of view, all graphics processing performance is made locally on the local computer to which the Head-mounted display (HMD) is connected with the processing power of the Graphics Processing Unit (GPU). All interaction between the players and the sound is transmitted through the server in the cloud, supported by STEAM services. So one of the critical points and reducing the chance of technical glitches during use is cloud hosting and lowering the threshold requirements for the user.

Alongside the required equipment, I provided recommended

specifications for the type of computer and its parts that customers were required to purchase. All the list of best practice settings was sent to the users to be most effective for operation without glitches. Most settings were sound and graphics optimization and Windows system security settings. In some cases, various plug-ins have been required to support the software. At the end of each installation, speed connection tests to the server and communication tests between the participants and the cloud were performed. All of these ensured a minimum of glitches in the connection performance.

As for the durability of the virtual reality helmet, I recommend choosing the HTC VIVE PRO helmet after three years of experience that preceded this project. I examined many parameters, such as the installation process, ease of operation for the user, unexpected low faults and troubleshooting documentation, sound quality in the internal microphone, sound quality in the device headphones, and low chance of hardware malfunctions even when the user causes unintentional damage. In addition, more complex parameters were examined, such as adjusting the distance of lenses between the eyes (adjustable for most users), maintenance costs for several years, repair complexity and spare parts, and more. I have learned from previous projects that hardware failure and hardware mismatch with the customer are critical in adopting the technology. It also affects the quality of the end-user experience. Therefore, before starting work, I emphasized the final application process in the field, which is an integral part of the work process planning.

2.1.4.3 REAL-LIFE EXPERIENCE

What makes the user feel that he is experiencing the experience that is closest to reality? What environmental factors must be produced to give it this feeling?
Furthermore, what realistic and imaginary environment do we know to create for the end user today?

2.1.4.3.1 INTUITIVENESS AND USER CONVENIENCE

Making the content accessible is necessary to create a comfortable technological environment for the user. A user who receives technology and has difficulty operating it will have difficulty connecting to the activity even if its content is valuable. For a first-time user, I suggest a tutorial that means the user's entry ticket into the virtual reality world. In the Tutorial I have developed with my team, the user is asked to perform several simple tasks in voice guidance in which he sees the controllers, and on them are marked all the buttons with a detailed explanation about the use. This is equivalent to when it was necessary to explain to the employees what the Internet is and how it may help them streamline and produce value in various processes.

2.1.4.3.2 INTERACTION WITH THE TRAINER

One of the most profound problems created in online learning is the feeling of lack of instruction from students, the feeling of non-interactive lecture, most of the time it takes staring at the screen for an hour and a half in front of the same frame, in some cases screen presentation of a presentation. Many students stated that the physical presence of a facilitator would improve their understanding and level of interest in the content.

We, therefore, chose that the trainer will be present in the experience and not outside of it. The facilitator within the experience has an essential role in activating the various activities and answering "face-to-face" questions in virtual reality. This point is important on two levels, one on the trainer's side, who feels he is as effective as he was before in the classroom, he also feels the fundamental technological change and the way to transfer the knowledge, but this process does not detract from its value and training as expressed by several lecturers (Lassoued et-al., 2020)

2.1.4.3.3 REAL-TIME

While at conferences, lecturers preferred to record the lecture and broadcast it edited afterward, in VR metaverse, people are given the option to be freer from standing in front of a camera and behave in the same way they were used to standing in front of an audience to lecture and guide. Live performance is an integral part of the interaction and sense of belonging to an active and energetic group that asks questions, works together, and does not feel like watching a playlist of pre-made videos. Real-time is an essential tool for trainees. The pace and dynamics differ between the trainer and the trainees, allowing much more relevant information to be transferred to the group since the trainer can adjust the content concerning the level of interest of the trainees and receive feedback on the level of listening.

2.1.4.3.4 NEUTRALIZING ENVIRONMENTAL DISTRACTIONS

One of the major problems nowadays during interviews, social gatherings, and even professional training is concentration. Using a mobile phone, environmental noises, sources of interest from the environment, notifications from IoT (Internet of things) devices, and more make us turn our attention to external events and make it difficult for us to perform a task. When using a virtual reality HMD, all distractions can be neutralized and thus draw the user's attention solely to the content we want him to see. The user is even imprisoned in a sense. Although he is given many choices in a virtual environment, all are carefully pre-selected by the programmers who built the scene and the story for him. This move is extreme by completely disconnecting the user from the environment. However, as part of the tools available to us in VR media, we have deliberately chosen to eliminate all distractions since we only achieve a high value of learning and concentration in tasks and increase user knowledge.

2.1.4.3.5 A REAL TANGIBLE ENVIORNMENT

To create an effective virtual environment and perform training in that environment, it is appropriate that the virtual environment reflects the real world as much as possible.
Much of creating the realistic feel is an architectural duplication of a real environment (a digital twin). There are types of training where the replication element is less critical. If there is no perfect copying of the environment, the training is ineffective, mainly in the security and industrial sectors.

2.1.4.3.6 SHARING INFORMATION BETWEEN PARTICIPANTS

According to Correia, Baran & Yusop (2007), there is an importance to the quality of the experience and the level of learning, which is expressed, among other things, in the group support and knowledge sharing between the users. Planning the experience in the form of mini-games in which each game includes teamwork or competitiveness so that at the end of each game, the outcomes are visible to all players and can be discussed. Valuable knowledge gained for the whole team, whether the user scored the most points. Also, the trainer who is part of the experience and other users can support each other during the experience and help acquire knowledge through learning by doing.

2.1.4.3.7 BRIDGING LANGUAGE GAPS

To maximize the technology potential, we can use digital tools and let the users see and accrue knowledge in the user's mother tongue. The language gap is accessible in a sophisticated way in which each user sees the task in his language. At the same time, he performs the activity with a person who speaks a different language in a multiplayer virtual location with a multi-lingual space. When the translation system is built into the system, adding different languages and bridging the language gap is easier. At a higher level, it can be done with Artificial Intelligence (AI) and spoken language, not only written (more details on that method in the summary section).

2.1.4.3.8 PERSONAL SCORE TO EVALUATE ACHIEVEMENTS

A significant gap I found during the literature review is the need for more to evaluate the performance. In addition to the participant's name and digital representation in space, adding a scoreboard where the participant accumulates an automatic score for positive actions he performs in the virtual space. So that at the end of the activity, administrators can objectively evaluate the user's contribution to the group or personal score on the tasks he had to perform.

Another significant advantage of the digital environment is that data collection can be performed so that each interaction is logged in a file and analyzed. Meaning, that at the end of a session, we can know exactly what the user interacts with, if it is a task or even what he watched, and how much he spoke and quickly can evaluate the performance.

To summarize this section of gaps and suggestions- all of those parameters I stated were part of my decisions in more than 100 different programs I developed with my team in the last six years and made a significant value by raising the user's immersion. By gaining more immersion, we achieve a more valuable experience for the user.

Based on my team's previous development experience, I presented how we decided to close gaps. However, many technical decisions have been made in addition to the details in the last section. I decided to assign this a separate technical article explaining the development decisions. Decisions that are not in this article: Implementing videos, adjusting the graphics level to hardware, optimizing the environments, selecting the functionality of the buttons on the controllers, computational methods to reduce software weight, user restrictions to prevent system crashes, methods of lowering system resources and other decisions made in the development process.

2.2 WHY DO BUSINESSES AND ORGANIZATIONS NEED TO TRANSFORM INTO VR METAVERSE

Virtual Reality enables users to experience new products, spaces, and possibilities in ways that are never possible. Brands and businesses can now take their products and services into 3D worlds populated by real people. The Metaverse can create more immersive and interactive communication between brands and customers. This VR metaverse will allow brands to interact with customers on a new level. It will be the foundation for all future immersive, interactive, and experiential advertising.

There are many reasons why businesses should take the first steps into the Metaverse and explore the evolving market. First, remember that many huge companies invest large sums of money in establishing the industry and introducing the technology and concept to the final consumer. For example, Microsoft acquired the gaming company Activision-Blizzard, a sign of Microsoft's entry into multiplayer experiences using gamification, and also considered investments in the HoloLens glasses on the hardware side. Nvidia is a company that develops tools for the industry to build metaverses and artificial intelligence models to facilitate the development process and implementation of the tools on various platforms. Ultimately, if a massive group of companies wants to lead, that change will happen. There are many examples, but the principle is that if huge companies lead change, businesses must learn and understand these moves even if they think they are wrong.

I will divide the reasons for performing digital transformation into two categories. (1) one within an organization and (2) two outside the organization (customer side).

It is important to note that only some industries need to adopt all approaches, and likewise, there are industries and organizations that the solutions will meet in a few years and not at this stage. At the internal organizational level, I expect that organizations will carry out a digital transformation to VR Metaverse to achieve the following:

2.2.1 WITHIN AN ORGANIZATION

We will also explore how the VR metaverse can be leveraged within an organization. We will analyze the prominent use cases of the VR metaverse, including virtual meetings, training, and collaboration. While there are numerous potential applications of VR metaverse within organizations, we will focus on the most common and impactful use cases. It is important to note that new and innovative use cases for VR metaverse within organizations will emerge as the technology continues to evolve. Therefore, this section provides a snapshot of current best practices. However, it is not exhaustive, and the possibilities for VR metaverse within organizations will continue to expand.

2.2.1.1 ONBOARDING

A fast and efficient onboarding process will save resources, shorten onboarding time, and better prepare the employees for a real-life situation than theory studies. One of the main problems in graduating in practical disciplines such as nursing is assessing the level of readiness of the graduates for the real world. It is estimated that the preparation of graduates in virtual reality to deal with stressful situations and the use of medical tools will increase the graduates' readiness level and thus improve the service to the patient. As a result, millions of dollars will be saved on field training and costs associated with the lack of professionalism of personnel in the field (Zackoff et al.,2020). An effective onboarding process teaches employees about the organizational culture, the hierarchy, and the vision. Employees who go through a positive process will come to the organization with higher motivation. Furthermore, a higher motivation will affect his marginal contribution to the company's activity, and the more the organization will generate a return on investment from the process

(Taylor,2005).

Sometimes the onboarding process in organizations requires practical experience from the employee, such as in the fields of security, rescue, and medicine, where the organization invests many resources in creating the simulation, which include investing in renting spaces, scenery, actors, consumables, and more. The use of multi-participant virtual reality can significantly reduce costs, eliminate the need for simulation areas and bring value to the organization's side in saving resources and streamlining the process, as well as better practical training for the employee since the simulation processes can include a digital twin of the same simulation area that will be more familiar to the employee later on and the employee Will arrive at the work area more prepared and efficient (Zackoff et-al,20202).

2.2.1.2 TRAINING AND SOFT SKILL

The field of training in virtual reality is a flourishing field. It is not new and may be among the oldest. One of the first applications ever made in virtual reality by NASA in the 1960s prepared the astronauts for a computerized environment that simulated a training environment in space (McGreevy, 1993). The technology was very limited, and immersive sensations were unavailable in those days. Still, with all the limitations, there was an understanding that virtual reality tutorials and training could make the medium's value more accurate. Furthermore, get the best out of it using simulated environments. Virtual environments enable the simulation of real environments or environments that cannot be produced in the real world.

The world of training is loaded with wasted money on many resources, including trainers' human resources, production of environments similar to a show or film, consumables, preparation time, space limitations, transportation of trainees to the designated training locations, and more.

Besides the tremendous savings in these resources, it is possible to produce a high educational value compared to traditional methods, so in a previous study I conducted with a research colleague as part of a grant from the European Union in the HORIZON 2020 project, we examined the values and reactions of a focus group after correctional officers performed training in prisons modeled according to architectural drawings. The results showed that about 80% of the participants stated that the method of acquiring knowledge in virtual reality using the learning-by-doing method was more effective, and the levels of interaction between the participants were higher than in traditional training. Also, they maintained the concentration of the participants when performing the task (Tubul-Lavy & Bianchi, 2021).

The training can occur in all market segments, from soft skills to providing emergency first aid. Many studies have been conducted on the value of virtual reality training.
Rakesh (2018) cites comparative studies that indicate some test cases for improving skills. For example, doctors who were trained in virtual reality made 40% fewer mistakes than doctors who were trained traditionally. The American Walmart chain conducted training for store managers in dealing with Black Friday and presented a success of 80% savings in training times. Also, United Rentals allows its representatives to bring the training environment from the field to the office, thus reporting a reduction of training times by 40%.

A model by Deloitte (2018) diagnoses when guidance and training in virtual reality can achieve the most value. In the model, a method is proposed in which the complexity of acting must be analyzed and, at the same time, the requirement at the level of knowledge acquisition, is it enough to act alone, or is it necessary to do a deep analysis and draw conclusions. If the operation is simple, there is no obligation to do the training in VR. If the operation is complex or requires in-depth analysis from the trainee, transferring the training to virtual reality makes sense.

Training in VR receives much support from many studies that indicate dramatic positive data in adopting virtual reality technologies in training. One of the most impressive results is the effectiveness of the training, which has multiplied four times concerning classroom studies and 1.5 times compared to other technological learning (Eckert & Mower, 2020). One of the most critical conclusions from the study shows a sharp increase of almost four times in the feelings and emotions involved during activity in virtual reality.

2.2.1.3 ON-LOCKATION TRAINING - INDUSTRIAL FACILITIES

In the industrial market, the internal use of virtual reality allows employees to experience complex technical processes and to consume the knowledge and practice as a meaningful experience in which many skills are also acquired (Andaluz el-al, 2018). As a result, the employees are interested in consuming more information and training and increasing the quality of the employee and his contribution to productivity in the company. In this way, routine maintenance of a power plant can be carried out in virtual reality and maintain the competence of employees to perform routine tasks (Shamsuzzoha el-al, 2021).

The implementation of processes of this type is a continuation of the transformation processes of factories to industry 4.0. Intelligent factories use virtual reality tools for training, carry out routine activities on the production floor, and produce work in the factory remotely (Alpala et al., 2022). Operating factories remotely using virtual reality is still in its infancy. Still, I foresee a growing trend in demand for applications in industries and examining the implementation of virtual reality processes on an ongoing basis. This process is also known as DIGITAL TWIN. A digital twin is a virtual representation of a physical object or system. It is a digital model used to simulate a physical object's real-world characteristics and behaviors, such as a building or a piece of machinery.

Digital twins are typically used for various purposes, such as design and engineering, manufacturing, testing and validation, and even remote monitoring and control of the physical object, as described above. The main advantages of the digital twin are the ability to train operators without wasting resources but still give them the feeling that they have performed the task in the real thing, monitor the plant or machine in real time, study data in real-time, and control the effects of changes in the model before making changes in the production process or the machine, performing complex optimizations for the entire supply chain (Pérez et-al, 2020). A significant percentage of the leading companies in the American economy stated that they are in the process of assimilating VR technologies (30%). In comparison, another 21% have already integrated virtual reality into their strategy (1004 companies participated in the sample) (Eckert & Mower, 2020). It is difficult to predict precisely how virtual reality digital twins will look in the future, as technology is constantly evolving and advancing. However, virtual reality digital twins will likely become more realistic and immersive, allowing users to experience a more lifelike digital representation of a physical space or object.

Additionally, virtual reality technology will likely become more widely available and affordable, making it more accessible to a broader range of users. Virtual reality digital twins will also be used for various applications, such as training, education, architecture, engineering, construction, healthcare, transportation, and entertainment. Soon, we will see changes in the human resources

skills required for these processes if, on the one hand, these processes can result in the dismissal of unqualified personnel. On the other hand, a worker will be trained to understand the operating procedure of a digital twin.

2.2.1.4 INTERNATIONAL TEAMWORK

In the previous section, we dealt with a digital twin, which is just a part of all the options in international teamwork. Despite using digital devices during the interaction between the users, we can still notice situations in which the emotional reaction is equal to the emotional reaction if they met for teamwork in reality. (Davis& Pledger, 2022).

Practicing working in teams is an important tool and is essential mainly in jobs that require high skill and communication between team members. For example, in medicine, teamwork is critical to patient treatment success. However, team training is also limited due to the limitations of the space that needs to be allocated in the operating rooms and experience in the field, as well as the difficulty in practicing teams on real people that may cause them significant damage and even death. Therefore, practicing teamwork in virtual environments can significantly contribute to the performance of work and team practice in virtual environments (Pavia et al., 2018) Furthermore, international knowledge sharing will help organizations transform the collective knowledge of individuals into organizational knowledge that helps to improve processes and preserve knowledge for passing it on to future generations (Yang, 2007). The abilities are inherent in international teamwork that different models and different cultures influence can expose teams to broader approaches in practical work and increase the wealth of accumulated knowledge. In other applied fields, such as engineering, team activity in virtual reality shows better performance, mainly in implementation, communication skills between team members, and the ability to solve problems. The planning phase Verbal and practical communication are significantly affected due to the ease of planning in a virtual environment equivalent to working together in the same space in the real world and the tools available to the learners. (Halabi, 2020). Collaboration in virtual environments also significantly shortens the time needed to design products. The presence in the virtual

world, regardless of the physical location, allows at any point in time to work in full collaboration, equivalent to an office work meeting (Kan et-al., 2001). It is possible to notice the significant power of teamwork even before light devices came into our lives for an immersive experience.

Back in 1997 (Lehner & DeFanti) it was found that teamwork in virtual reality technologies bridged time and place gaps and enabled the work of car design between a team from the United States and Belgium. Today, when technology advances, teams in all fields can meet and produce collaborative work from anywhere. Studies in the field of construction offer a solution in virtual work environments that will later eliminate the need for planners and designers to work in the field and give them advantages in working remotely in the virtual environments and even make it easier for them the planning operations that are sometimes more difficult in the field than in the multi-user virtual environment (Zaker & Coloma, 2018).

2.2.2 OUTSIDE THE ORGANIZATION

At the customer level, brands and businesses will have to provide customers with experiences at a higher threshold of excitement and interactive experiences that will constitute the next stage of the Internet. After 30 years of using the Internet with different platforms, customers demand a renewal of the language and the way they consume knowledge and brands. I can spot where it begins, but I can only assess what devices and case studies we will have in the future using virtual worlds. The future will be enjoyable, and we will all wait to see what the creative minds of the creators will bring to the market.

2.2.2.1 NEW BRANDING AND ADVERTISING OPTIONS

The world of advertising and brands has been resurrected. The coming years will go through complex processes of recognizing a new language and understanding the new opportunities available to advertisers. On the employment side, new roles and expertise will be created in each field, as happened in the WEB 2.0 era when the first website was published in 1991 and began to disrupt the world of online advertising. It took time, but no one knew what the future held for us back then. No websites, search engines, social networks, or SAAS platforms existed. Furthermore, in this period, we are experiencing a new era that will allow existing or new brands to enter the market with full force through branding and marketing methods.

Embedding virtual products into environments and experiences is a tool equivalent to covert advertising in movies or TV shows. In every experience, the user can borrow elements from the real world. Although the field is not new, and computer games are increasingly used to implement the method, we are experiencing a resurgence of many virtual worlds that are not necessarily from the gaming field.

Many ideas will come up in the coming years, but the potential of virtual events is clear. Sponsorships for virtual events will be a tool for producers and organizations to receive payment for the production of the events. At the same time, advertisers will be happy to sponsor events where accurate information can be obtained for the audience that will attend. The sponsorship for events in the virtual world can change the way the sponsorship is given and not necessarily place a sign in the style of "Your logo here." the virtual sponsorships can be wearing avatars in company logo shirts, distributing virtual accessories on behalf of the advertiser, interactive experience rooms for preferred audience groups and multi-participant group competitions on the company's products. Virtual events differ from physical events in that the event's space is not limited, so there is no limit to the number of people. In theory, virtual events can take place 24/7 with an audience of millions worldwide.

Influencers, models, and celebrities who want to continue their existence and influence in the virtual worlds will have to build for themselves the avatar that will represent them in the campaigns. The avatars will be able to represent the influencer indefinitely, and he will not be required to be photographed for campaigns again. Using artificial intelligence will teach the influencer's voice, and he will not be required to come to photo shoots. Someday, influencers will only demand to sell their rights to an avatar that will continue to exist and work in the virtual world without them.

2.2.2.2 REACHING NEW TARGET AUDIENCES OF GENERATION Z AND ALPHA

Marketers are now forced to get creative and find new ways to reach their target audiences. They constantly look for new ways to make their content more immersive and interactive. Currently, the most popular way is to create a 3D world that acts as a digital environment for the audience. The Metaverse can change how we interact with brands and businesses. It will allow us to explore new worlds and experience things in ways that were not possible before. Generation Z is better known for being technologically savvy and having an entrepreneurial mindset. The Gen Z group had over 360$ billion of income to spend and invest, which makes them very lucrative customers with massive potential for growth (Pollard, 2021). The impact of Metaverse on brands and businesses is enormous. It provides them with an opportunity to reach new target audiences.

Reaching target audiences from the Z and Alpha generations - these generations were born into the virtual world, and their abilities and digital orientation are much higher than the previous generations. Therefore they exist in the virtual worlds and tend to adopt technologies and opportunities in these worlds more easily. These generations learn alone on the Internet and rely on (sometimes unreliable) visual information. These generations acquire professions in the virtual worlds and develop an avatar persona.

They will try to stand out in any way, even if it is extroverted and extreme, to gather fans and followers. The activity in the virtual worlds allows these generations to also break through the limits of bureaucracy and allow themselves to perform actions that bypass government, such as creating undeclared capital, generating profits from virtual currencies, providing services such as 3D modeling, creating wallets, orientation, and consulting for generations Y and X, NO CODE services in artificial intelligence that are not accessible to older generations and many more services.

The potential in entering the virtual world is raising brand awareness for younger generations, not necessarily brands we would think these generations would consume. According to the BOF (October 2022) data, Nike is the most talked about and loved brand by these generations, followed by the Gucci brand (which generally does not connect with the values of the younger generations). It should be noted that in 2021 Nike purchased the startup RTFKT for a billion dollars, which produces 3D models as NFT. This step seemed to be an integral part of the younger generation's sympathy for Nike. These generations lead the values of creation, information sharing, anti-regulation, and a desire to return data control to their hands. Therefore, they tend to create private events with the artists they like who lead the values they belong to. In addition, these generations have significant consumption power since they generate income for themselves. They also own a significant amount of virtual currencies they must spend, only sometimes according to the law and tax reports. These generations tend to invest in virtual rather than tangible assets, thus creating another market. Some sources claim that Generation Z owns most virtual currencies due to their familiarity with the technology and entering this field at the right time. Practical examples of the activity of brands to touch the consciousness of these generations are Balenciaga, Ralph Lauren, and Lacoste, who knew how to team up with game brands and produce joint content in some of the most popular games ever released, such as Fortnite and Roblox.

2.2.2.3 OPENING NEW INTERNATIONAL - AUDIENCES

The elements of playfulness and experience characterize the virtual worlds, and most do not require an understanding of written or spoken language. The common denominator is trying to remove barriers and allow as many people as possible to enjoy shared experiences. The virtual worlds make it possible to reach a broad target audience, broader than what is usually thought of as a brand. In the past, brands used to base their audience and relationships on customers according to a profile they built for the product and the brand. The target audience comprised items with a known common denominator in advance. In the virtual worlds, we can find the same target audience mixed in the same experiences with different audiences that we did not think would be exposed to the brand and even become potential customers. The background of the target audiences is different and diverse, and it will be challenging to distinguish the correct target populations in the future. Consumers of all generations and all ages purchase products on the entire price scale and are independent of geographic area.

In most cases, the global world eliminates the focus on geographic groups since the products can reach anywhere by shipment, and shortly many products will be digital. For example, in the past, it was customary to sell software on discs and send it to customers. Over the years, the discs have moved to download software from the net, and so has the evolution of books that go from intricate print to E BOOKs that are sent to customers. Many products exist only virtually, such as songs, photos, wearable accessories for avatars in games, points, and Virtual money within games, bank transfers, and more. Everything in evolution that succeeds in going digital will be sold and reach a broader customer base following thevirtual worlds.

2.2.2.4 SALES OF VIRTUAL ACCESSORIES

Use of technologies to establish a unique exclusiveness for the products. The technologies make it possible to give an agreed confirmation between all participants about the uniqueness of digital products. Thus, for example, a person who owns a digital image will be able to receive the recognition that he is the owner of the original image and it is in his possession. Even if there are copies of the work on the net (and there will be), everyone will still agree that one person holds the original image with the digital signature. This is just one of many uses I will detail about the blockchain technology that allows using NFT, NON-FUNGIBLE TOKEN, a currency that cannot be exchanged. All users about the ownership of that virtual object agree upon a single- valued notation that cannot be changed. It can be a song, a picture, a digital file, virtual real estate or non-virtual real estate (as registered in the municipality), car ownership, a fraud detection tool for the authenticity of objects, signing documents, ownership of safes, and more. I will not go into an explanation of the technology itself, but the use of everything is accessible to everyone and, in most cases, does not require knowledge of the code. Using existing tools in the network tries to make the technology accessible to everyone. Due to the misuse of technology in recent years and the law's ambiguity on these issues, people are reluctant to experiment in the field and wait for the technology and the law to mature further. One way or another, even without blockchain technology, products are purchased with real money. For example, cars worth hundreds of millions of dollars in the USA are sold yearly in the virtual worlds with the Vroom platform (start beyond,2021). Mc'donalds claims people will eventually hang out and buy food and beverages through their metaverse platform (marr,2022).

2.2.2.5 VIRTUAL EVENTS

The world of virtual events is gaining momentum due to unique elements that make it very attractive to the worlds of sales and showrooms. Since the Corona outbreak, virtual events have become necessary due to the limitations of movement and social distancing. People have realized that many things can be done with a physical meeting, although it can be seen that it is only possible to replace 100% physical meetings.

Online sales events are not new, and there are quite a few online sales events limited in time, whether it is newsletters selling products for a limited time, a stock clearance week, sales towards the end of a calendar year to empty warehouses, sales for a limited time before holidays and the examples are many more. In the virtual worlds, they found additional advantages beyond the gap of the meeting location. The experience in the virtual worlds is the closest experience to reality. It offers a meeting of avatars that can exist in real-time with the ability to move between private and public areas to create a world that matches the real world in experience, the feeling of presence and belonging to that event. Unlike with zoom, for example, you put a camera on a black screen, and it is doubtful whether you are at an event or busy with other things. The virtual world is full of interactions, walking and moving between rooms and the world of content, an open microphone, and a sound experience of distance from the objects as in the real world, suddenly there is a meaning to the location of the avatar in the world in relation to the virtual stage, to the (virtual) contact between the characters, the possibility of producing an event without space limitations, without insurances, without the logistics of electricity, meals, setting up stands, expenses of suppliers on printing and physical transportation of equipment, but to take advantage of the full potential of event ticket revenues, sponsorships and a value proposition for customers, as well as accessibility and the possibility of opening the events to any desired scale, now A local store can produce huge events that will not embarrass the tech giants that do annual physical events.

The tools available to exhibitors at events of this type sometimes give them a higher value than an actual event, saving resources and even displaying products they could not present in the real world. Imagine a customer who, until today, would come to a conference where there would be a 2 square meter booth and hand out brochures to sell the products of the cosmetics factory His now will be able to take a potential customer on an interactive, experiential journey not limited in time or place and allow the customer to visit the factory, see the product line and even assemble his product basket. The customer journey has changed for the benefit of business owners, and now the sales process is much more moment and experience-driven so that we can see beautiful ideas in the coming years for how marketing creates value for its customers and offers to sell its merchandise. For example, in September 2021, the luxury fashion company MONCLER created a virtual event to expand the possibility of designers from all over the world participating if it has been held so far in Milan (Clark,2021).

2.2.2.6 BRANDING AND POSITIONING "HERE I AM"

Finally, the marketing side also has a significant value for many companies that want to be perceived as innovative and unique. Even with the actual value still unclear and what each side will gain from the connection to the virtual worlds, the mere statement of an innovative organization in the virtual worlds is a statement towards the customers. Just as every organization owns a virtual asset of FB, INSTAGRAM, TIKTOK, and more, it also needs to own a virtual world that will make a mark and say, "we are here too." Organizations of this type will gain experience in the field, feel the terrain, learn the clientele, and shortly know how to take advantage of the virtual asset and improve it according to the organization's needs and its agenda. Many organizations failed to provide value to their customers on the first attempt, but they learned the different platforms and got to know the new tools to stand out and reach different target audiences. Each platform has its language and way of standing out, its embedded trends, and the successful campaigns that make the difference. As organizations have learned the world of SEO, they will have to learn the language of the new virtual worlds.

2.3 THE PROBLEM
AND PROCESS INHIBITORS

Virtual environments in all their shades have reached a point where the market has shown a willingness to adopt the technology and the concept in all areas of life. The market is conceptually ready for significant change and disruption in our lives. The technology is mature enough to start a process of penetration into households, and the public relations for the Metaverse vision keep the vibe in the headlines. However, businesses may face some potential challenges and issues when using Metaverse.

2.3.1 LIMITED ADOPTION

According to the Metaverse vision, one must have costly equipment in order to have the most immersive experience and assimilate into the content. Most of the simple glasses sold to the final consumer are based on a low-level chip that allows the use of good content. This type of HMD is called Stand-alone. It can stand independently and allow users to experience virtual environments without connecting to a computer or using additional accessories.

However, to allow content at a graphic level and high interaction, the user must use an HMD connected to a computer based on a graphics card. Which also enables interfaces for immersive accessories such as sensing suits or synchronizing objects from the real world to the virtual one. For these reasons, businesses that want to turn to the world of Metaverse but need help get their hands on a specific focus group with a common denominator.

2.3.2 COMPLEXITY

Designing and developing VR metaverse platforms is complex and unlike web worlds. The complex technical knowledge required for these platforms includes many capabilities that are not yet accessible to the public as accessible tools without the need to use code. The range of skills includes understanding user experience design in games, design, and modeling of 3D virtual worlds, a concept design for characters and animations, storytelling, cloud services, artificial intelligence, data analysis, compliance with privacy protection standards, and complex architectures built for user load. The involvement of many factors makes the task difficult for small businesses or design studios and requires the investment of many resources. Also, since there is no uniform standard, even if there is a relatively accessible platform, it will probably work according to the protocol it created. That is not necessarily the right and good thing.

2.3.3 SECURITY AND PRIVACY CONCERNS

The virtual worlds are part of the Internet and, like any platform, suffer from breaches in information security that keep developing over the years. The METAVERSE will suffer from several other issues that must be considered beyond the security problems known from web platforms.

Phishing scams - over time, fraudulent methods of this type will develop in cyberspace, and hackers will use the users' innocence and reveal sensitive information from them in a conversation between avatars or in transferring data in an interaction that did not exist on the web and email worlds.

Identity theft is a genuine concern as any user can create avatars with tools based on a photo from the web today. If that is not enough, artificial intelligence tools now allow learning and using a person's voice without permission. Voice recognition and other biometric authentication methods are no longer effective, and security levels and misuse prevention must be considered.

Biometric tracking, such as Eye-tracking technologies, hand tracking, and biometric metrics, including movement and sense, are becoming popular in advanced HMDs. On the one hand, improving the user experience, making the experience more immersive, and improving the graphics performance are possible. On the other hand, the technology will allow corporations to collect sensitive biometric information about the user, unlike a password - the latter cannot be changed. Some of the data also includes taking pictures of the pupils, and if a database of this type is hacked, we can try and assess the massive damage that can be caused.

Sexual harassment, unfortunately, is not a new topic on the Internet. Still, how it is carried out in the metaverse worlds can raise a level since it is possible to enter the private space of any avatar in the virtual worlds and make contact without going through particular filtering or approval from both parties. Today, there is a lack of tools for operators to reduce and prevent harassment in virtual worlds. In the virtual world, hands are used, and an unrestricted verbal manner is more similar to an actual face-to- face meeting experience and may pose an equally real threat.

2.3.4 LEGAL ISSUES

The new space is mainly unregulated. The existing laws that apply online are still being determined to be realized in the virtual world, which will raise new legal issues due to the new tools and language it offers. Uncertainties can also make it difficult for developers of virtual worlds and platforms, who can be exposed to lawsuits and changing regulations that can cause them to collapse immediately. Some issues that may challenge the law are copyright violations of works such as using images, sound, video, and three-dimensional elements from around the web. Challenges regarding virtual crimes in the virtual space that are not associated with a geographical area are now the responsibility of the platform owners. Due to the WEB 3.0 approach, we run into additional complex issues since the concept is that the platform belongs to the users, and they are the ones who manage and create. If this is the case, who will be responsible for prosecution?

The gray areas are also used by tax criminals, gambling, and illegal businesses that will take advantage of the grace period when there is no precise regulation to launder money or make a fortune through the virtual worlds.

As I wrote in previous sections, data collection is increasing. Therefore, the regulation will have to promote legislation on how organizations collect biometric information. Will rights organizations strongly oppose the collection of this type of data?

2.3.5 TIME-CONSUMING

Metaverse environments are complex. The development of the environment depends on many factors that require time and resources. The size of the environment will affect the precious time it will take to build many 3D elements and virtual assets to cover all areas. Thinking about the concept of the experience and writing storytelling will also affect the time (beyond the financial resource). Embedding characters and animations will require additional teams and time to create the avatars according to the required concept, clothing, and styling accessories. Cracking the purpose of building the experience is no less critical. Developing a gaming experience is not equivalent to an educational experience or a branded experience. Additional time will be required in the characterization stages to determine the nature of the experience and the goals.

Metaverse infrastructure is complex and cannot compare to setting up a website. A comprehensive cloud infrastructure should handle user connection, visual processing, data collection, and many other tasks in real-time. Establishing a metaverse environment can take several months, depending on the project's complexity.

2.3.6 NO PROTOCOLS

One challenge identified in the metaverse development is the need for a standard protocol or set of rules that all parties can agree on and follow. This can make it difficult for different virtual worlds and systems to interoperate and communicate with each other, limiting the metaverse's potential and making it harder for users to move between different virtual spaces. It can also make it difficult for developers to create new applications and services that can be used in the metaverse, as they may need to support various protocols and standards. In general, developing standards and protocols for the metaverse is an active area of research and development. Several different groups, organizations, and standards bodies are involved in this process.

These groups may develop standards for various areas, including 3D graphics, virtual reality, virtual currencies, identity, security, and more.

2.3.7 VERSITES COMPARING WEBSITES AND SOCIAL MEDIA

Building a metaverse environment is similar to building a website in some ways, but it is also significantly different in other ways. Building a metaverse environment like a website involves designing and developing content and functionality and implementing technical infrastructure to support it. It also requires ongoing maintenance and updates to keep the environment functioning smoothly and effectively.

However, several key differences exist between building a website and a metaverse environment. One of the main differences is the level of complexity involved. Building a metaverse environment typically requires specialized technical expertise and much more advanced development than building a website. It also creates virtual assets, such as 3D models and animations, which are not typically required to develop a website.

Another key difference is the level of interactivity and immersion. A metaverse environment is designed to be a fully immersive and interactive virtual space, while a website is typically a more passive platform for information and communication. Building a metaverse environment involves designing and implementing various interactive features and functionality, which is not typically required in developing a website.

The metaverse is similar to social media in some ways, as both online platforms allow users to connect and communicate. There are, however, significant differences between them as well. The metaverse is the platform for interactivity between avatars and extends the reality capabilities, and contains immersive technology such as virtual reality and augmented reality supported by the internet infrastructure. It is designed to be a fully immersive and interactive virtual environment, enabling real-time user communication and interaction.

In contrast, social media platforms are typically more passive for communication and information sharing and do not offer the same level of interactivity and immersion as the metaverse. While the metaverse provides the potential for fully immersive and interactive virtual experiences, social media platforms are typically more focused on communication and information sharing.

While the metaverse and social media have some similarities, they are also significantly different regarding their functionality and the experiences they offer users. It is challenging to accurately compare users' average time in the metaverse versus on websites. Metaverse development and adoption are still in their infancy, and data on usage patterns is limited. Additionally, the amount of time users spend in the metaverse or on websites will depend on various factors, including the content and functionality of the versite or website, the user's interests and goals, and the user's overall level of engagement with the platform.

The metaverse offers the potential for fully immersive and interactive virtual experiences, which can be more engaging and captivating for users than traditional websites. Users' time spent in the metaverse will vary based on various factors and differ from user to user. Users will likely spend more time in the metaverse than on websites.

Every business will have a metaverse presence as they have websites and social media, which is the significant potential of building tools to adapt the medium easily.

3. APPROACH AND SOLUTION

The following section proposes a new model for defining the significant parameters required to perform digital transformation effectively. This model addresses the challenges identified in the previous sections and provides organizations with a framework for successfully implementing digital transformation initiatives.

Additionally, a software solution is presented that helps organizations to assess their digital transformation readiness and identify areas for improvement. This software is specifically designed to address the market problem of designing a VR metaverse environment that meets users' needs. Finally, a case study demonstrates the benefits of using the proposed model and software in a real-world digital transformation process. The case study showcases how the new model and software were able to help an organization overcome critical challenges and achieve significant benefits from its digital transformation efforts. This section provides organizations with a practical framework and toolset for successful digital transformation initiatives.

3.1 5 I'S MODEL

As we continue to embrace and explore the potential of virtual worlds, we must consider how to build the best possible experience for users. The virtual reality metaverse, in particular, offers a unique opportunity to create immersive and interactive environments that can enhance business operations and customer engagement.

However, in our journey toward building these virtual worlds, it is essential to identify and address any gaps in the current media landscape. In this model, I aim to collect and analyze these gaps and provide insights on how the virtual reality metaverse can be leveraged to bridge these gaps and create a more impactful and meaningful experience for all stakeholders. My model is open and flexible, allowing new ideas and technologies to be incorporated as they emerge. I plan to guide businesses in transforming into the virtual world through a structured approach and a focus on relevant forms and sub-topics.

One of the key benefits of using this model for business transformation into the virtual world is the opportunity to minimize failures and maximize success. By analyzing and learning from over 150 previous projects and case studies, I have identified common pitfalls and challenges businesses may encounter when navigating this transition. By following the guidance in this model, businesses can avoid making the same mistakes and instead focus on building a solid foundation for their virtual operations.

In addition, using this model can save businesses time and money in the long run. By carefully planning and strategizing their transition into the virtual world, businesses can avoid costly errors and delays that can impact their bottom line. By following a structured approach and considering all relevant factors, businesses can make informed decisions that support their goals and objectives.

The potential of this model is to provide businesses with a reliable and tested method for successful transformation into the virtual world. By leveraging the insights and guidance provided, businesses can confidently navigate this transition and achieve their desired outcomes most efficiently and effectively as possible.

The "5 Is" model is a helpful framework for analyzing and planning digital transformation initiatives, particularly in the context of virtual worlds.

3.1.1 IMMERSION

According to the Cambridge dictionary, immersion is "the fact of becoming completely involved in something."

In our case - user involvement in the experience. Immersion has different levels, and they are determined not necessarily by the accessories and tools used by the user but by the subjective feeling of the user and the level of distractions that disconnect him from experience.

Generally speaking - the more a user is immersed in the experience, feels more senses, and connects emotionally to the content, the higher the level of immersion. The level of immersive affects the user to feel his presence within a simulation and experience the digital on a perceptual and emotional level as if he had gone through it in the physical world (Ryan, 1999). Does every experience need the highest level of immersion?

The short answer is no. Each experience should be developed with an orientation to how the user consumes and considering the other sections in this chapter that directly affect the balance. Consumption of an experience with a high level of immersion should be measured and controlled since the effect on the user's emotions and complete disconnection from the physical world can sometimes cause issues. Users may experience trauma or intense emotions in an unsupportive environment and end the experience with emotional harm. In addition, experiences at high immersive levels are very intense, flooded with stimuli for the brain, and last a short time that aims to be shorter than 30 minutes. Furthermore, different users react differently to stimuli.
Therefore, a high amount of stimuli will increase the likelihood of an unpleasant feeling for some users, manifesting in headaches, eye pain, dizziness, and sensory overload, leading to the end of

the experience earlier than expected. Can we control the senses through technology?

According to Özcan (2020), it is possible to influence each of the senses through technology. In his review, the writer divides the effects on sight, hearing, touch, smell, and taste.

Sight: Devices worn on the head with viewing screens are defined as Head Mounted Displays, or HMD for short, mainly used for virtual reality. However, other devices similar in appearance to semi-transparent glasses can be attributed to this category. In addition to the HMD, another technology that affects the sense of sight is known as a type of contact lens developed by the MOJO VISION company, which, as of these days, is not produced for customers. Among the leading companies in the market competing for the sense of sight are HTC, PICO, META, MICROSOFT, and Apple (sooner or later). In addition to viewing the screens, supporting technologies such as eye tracking can also be associated with the immersive level. Beyond collecting data on the user, eye tracking can also be used to improve the user's experience with rendering and display capabilities of the areas where the user concentrates and raise the graphic level.

I anticipate significant progress in the tools that affect the sense of sight since they are central to the experience. In most cases, achieving an immersive experience or combining additional tools is only possible with the first level of the sense of sight.

Hearing : the auditory aspect is part of the distraction and environmental disconnection tool. The basic level uses soundproof headphones with an environmental noise filtering mechanism that allows the user to avoid distractions and reactions from those around him during the activity. In this experience, the user is focused on the sounds emanating from the experience and is thus focused on instructions or music that can contain and affect emotions. Maintaining a private area in the virtual space gives the user a sense of security and helps him forget that he is in a physical area different from the experience. At the next level, it is possible to use spatial audio that can simulate spatial sound sources within the experience, which gives a different direction to the sound, draws the user's attention, and gives the user a sense of sound closer to the way they hear in reality. The highest level is ambisonic sound, a technology in which spatial sound can be recorded in a particular area and played the same way it was recorded. At this level, users can feel the sound, estimate the distance from which it comes and its direction, and thus react naturally to the environment in a way most similar to actual physical spaces (Rana et al., 2019).

Touch: the sense of touch is one of the most critical challenges in developing an immersive experience. This sense accompanies the experience on different levels. It gives feedback to the user, assists him in leading the experience, signals warnings to the user, and feeds the user complex feelings in the sounds of the various technological accessories. Each of the accessories affects a different sensing area and has elements of feeling at different levels. The challenge in developing these means is to achieve the transfer of the feeling, but at the same time to produce comfortable and easy-to-operate wearable accessories that will not interfere with the user's sense of presence in the experience while he is immersed in it.

Controllers- at the base of the experience, the user holds the game controls. Most of them include feedback of a slight vibration that can be felt when pressing a button, for example, to confirm the click of the user who, in most cases, does not see the controls due to how the HMD is used. In addition, if there is no other sensory wearable accessory, the remotes are the feedback for the sensations of touch during the experience. This is how users get a vibration indication when pressing buttons in the virtual world when meeting an avatar or any other mode of interaction with accessories or other users.

Body- During the last few years, several haptic vest suits equipped with different technologies have been released on the market with the same purpose, indicating sound and touch at different points on the user's body (Stone, 2001). Some wearable accessories convey the feeling by controlling different sound frequencies and bass strength, and some work with an SDK for developers who can set vibration and recoil in different places according to the content. For example, the developers can create solid and significant local feedback in the stomach area if a ball hits the avatar in a virtual soccer game. Other advanced wearable accessories can even affect the body's temperature and produce states of feeling cold and hot during an experience.

Seat and floor-Integrating technology for movement while exposed to visual content are not new. For years it has been possible to experience watching the cinema with the movement of a chair and the addition of vibrations. Motorized chairs corresponding to the observed scenes raise the sensory bar and create an additional stimulus that improves the user's connection to the experience. The user experiences a higher arousal than a visual experience alone (Pauna et al., 2018). In virtual reality, users would prefer to add vibration that matches the experience or sensory feedback To maintain arousal and interest in the experience (Li et al., 2021).

Smell: is one of the senses that few beliefs can be integrated into immersive experiences. Only a few studies have been written about integrating advanced scent technologies in virtual worlds. One of the factories in the USA with a vision of using the powers of scent to store memories bears the name OVR (Olfactory Virtual

Reality). The claim is that in the distant future, we will minimize static photographs and consume virtual experiences, where we can also

save the memory of the smell that will be able to remind us of the experiences in a better way (Wisniewski, 2019). The smell is a subjective matter. Therefore, using different smells in virtual worlds may affect users differently. The smell allows a person to assess the environment if it may contain positive elements, with smells of flowers, for example, or smells of sweet fruit, or even to smell danger by familiar smells (Ramic-Brkic & Chalmers, 2010). Simulation of smell is one of the senses that are more difficult to produce and apply correctly due to the subjective nature of this sense. Every study examining the conduction of a user in a virtual space with the help of smell sources found a similar result between the two groups examined (Nakamoto et al., 2020). From this, the integration of the sense of smell is still in its infancy, and so far, not many applications have been found in the field that has a significant impact. Nevertheless, the field of PTSD treatment in the exposure method finds the right place to apply smell. The tool Assists in the process and completes the exposure experience in that sense, which is challenging to transfer from the moments of trauma (Herz, 2021).

Taste: the least tested and applied sense in virtual environments due to the technological and physical limitations around it. Over the years, virtual reality devices and other accessories complement an immersive experience, become smaller and enable the combination of multiple senses at the same time. The sense of taste shares common spaces with the sense of smell, but when there is a real need to test the effect of tasting, the user must perform an active action of chewing or licking real food.

Studies in this field concluded a connection between the physical chewing of real food and the experience of chewing without real food (Hoffman et al., 1998). It feels like a natural consequence;

who would not prefer to eat real chocolate compared to an

equivalent experience without the chocolate? However, what if we examine the opposite effect on taste? Where the brain produces an experience of a change in the taste of the actual product through visual exposure. The study observed the use of this method in order to make it easier for children to taste bitter medicine through exposure to sweet contents. The study found a strong effect of

exposure to sweet content that prevented nausea after tasting a bitter medicine (Niki et al., 2021). It was also found that the judgment of our taste is affected by exposure to content in different environments.

Even though we taste the same substance, our opinion will change, and so will the variety of associations (Torrico et al., 2020). So the use of the sense of taste in itself is not extensive, but the visual effect on the human brain is undoubtedly a useful tool that can cause a change in the perception of taste. We hope to see in the market devices and technological capabilities to use the sense of taste while using virtual reality. Until then, we will observe an educated use of the influence on taste perception.

To conclude the immersion component, I found it appropriate to show the capabilities of technology's influence on the various senses and the tools available today. With the help of understanding the immersive component, we can make decisions about the connection and the relationship with the other components that I will review later. At the end of this chapter, the system of connections between the components will affect practical decision-making in the field.

3.1.2 INTERACTION

In virtual worlds, interaction is one of the most important and influential components. This component makes the experience more meaningful due to the wide variety of interactions it allows the user. The new medium's language allows almost all body parts to interact. Existence in the virtual space produces four central possibilities, which I will review for human-human and human-machine interfaces.

First, until now, we were used to how the user consumes a two-dimensional medium by touching a remote control or the screen. In the best case -technological way with hand gestures. When using technology such as virtual reality, the user must get to know and learn different and varied interface methods:

HMD - use of the helmet sensors and the direction of the gaze to the center of attraction or the interaction in the content. This way, the user turns the gaze and the distance from the desired object. With the help of the gaze, it is sometimes possible to select objects, confirm visibility or move forward in space.

Hand controls - a primary interface using the game controls that include several keys that allow users to mark points in the experience, jump from point A to B, open a menu, grab objects or people, and exit the application. The game controls are the closest tool to the keyboard and mouse, console game controls, or TV controls—the most intuitive interface on the list.

Voice commands- combined with artificial intelligence, it is possible to produce voice commands in virtual worlds to perform actions, similar to personal assistants such as Siri or Bixby. In voice-activated interfaces, users can create commands for assistance with movement, silencing other users, locking or opening rooms, creating accessories, selecting points of interest, and more.

Hand gestures- The new technologies in most of the devices on the market today support hand gestures. As in the mobile field, hand movements are a new field that calls for and expects standardization. Today, many companies produce different hand gestures to activate different features. Until there is standardization in the field, we can switch between different companies' devices, try different interfaces, and test our comfort level.

Eye interface - in advanced devices, eye tracking systems can be used to perform an activity in space. If there is tracking, then, there is also the option to extract and analyze information according to which the content will change according to the user's choices or to activate and deactivate modules on which the user focuses.

Brain-content interface - a high level of interaction with the content is influenced by thought. There are only a few devices that support the interface above. Users can find expensive devices or accessories that can be worn on an existing helmet and control the content with the help of thought. Users can communicate with the content with the help of mental control of the brain waves. For example, users can focus thinking, raise a specific wavelength, and cause a virtual object to float in space.

The increasingly near future ability to leave the interface of the game controls will revolutionize the user interface, a revolution similar to when the iPhone came out and eliminated the keys on the phone for all of us. We had to learn an interface that included tapping with fingers and various combinations, as well as hand gestures that allowed us to have a wide variety of interactions in less time and with greater ease.

Today, various interfaces are being discussed, which mainly

try to eliminate the experience of using game controls and move to the use of body interfaces and biological interfaces that can coexist and simultaneously eliminate the need to hold actual accessories in one's hands.

All interfaces refer to how the user can interact during the experience. The four types of interactions in the experience are interaction with menus, interaction with other players, interaction with objects in space, and interaction with artificial intelligence or computer- operated players. I will divide the interaction processes into four main parts directly affecting how experiences are developed.

3.1.2.1 INTERACTION WITH MENUS

These days there are many attempts to crack the best way for the user to interact with menus. Since there is no uniform standard for realizing menus and a familiar UI, various menu locations in the virtual space can be named. There are also many methods for opening the menu and marking choices. Some ways include several moves until reaching the player's choice, and some with the help of fewer moves with higher accessibility. For example, choosing the location of the settings menu and location have a wide range of options, from a fixed location in the corner of the screen to a James Bond-style menu opening interface. Part of the debate about how interactions should be done is through user feedback. New interfaces that are unfamiliar should go through an intermediate stage of a mixed interface between the known and familiar to the consumer and the advanced utopian interface that the consumer will most likely not recognize.

Building an interface similar to how the consumer consumes on other platforms may lose the value of intuitiveness in immersive interfaces. For example, using a three-bar menu (known as a hamburger) familiar to the WEB 2.0 interface may bother the user, who constantly sees the marking on the top side of the screen. In order to perform a basic microphone mute operation, the user will require: to open the interface, which is done by using the game remote control, opening a laser beam or another type of pointer (which replaces the role of the mouse), and selecting by pressing the TRIGGER button in most cases (which replaces the left mouse button) After that search for an internal menu of sound configuration control and from there another choice on "Mute." This whole complex process to please the customer and prevent him from a digital orientation process to an interface that includes a new language damages a fluid experience. A voice interface can easily replace the action; all the user has to do is say one word, "MUTE." Many processes in the menus are very complex since many personal processes have been added in multiplayer sessions, and the familiar keyboard and mouse are away from our service. In personal menus, we can find multiple options, including language adjustments, personal instructions, moving\teleporting to other areas of the experience, and many more. All this time, our avatar is exposed to the possibility of interaction with other users, and we must consider what happens with the virtual body while the mind is busy with choices. Questions to be raised while developing the interfaces are: Is the user's avatar available to engage with others? Does everyone see that the user is busy with a personal experience? Does the user's avatar even appear in the shared space when he is in another interaction that does not allow him additional interfaces? Can other players see his menu and personal preferences? Is there a possibility for the user to be in the personal menu and to continue other interfaces at the same time?

It should be noted that today most virtual worlds leave a bridge for the user to flow into the WEB 3.0 through familiar WEB 2.0 interfaces to make the selection and development processes more accessible for them. This registration process for the virtual worlds is carried out in the vast majority of cases through a recognized and well- known WEB interface. It includes one-click registration through Google and Apple accounts Or Facebook. The players' names, personal details, and information that may contain much text and open questions still find their place in using the keyboard and mouse due to the uncompromising convenience, preventing users from abandoning the log-in process. The dissonance between customer satisfaction and the implementation of a smooth transition between the interfaces and the full realization of the potential of the menu interfaces will accompany us for several more good years until the market education reaches a point where users will no longer be served in other ways. This can be paralleled to the appointment scheduling systems in various institutions that made scheduling a phone or internet appointment possible. Over time they closed the telephone centers, and the appointment scheduling systems remained in the application only. To this day, those who fail to adopt the technological method find themselves out of the game without possibly using the tools and the available language.

3.1.2.2 INTERACTION WITH OTHER PLAYERS

A meeting between avatars in virtual environments contains elements familiar to us from non-immersive virtual meetings such as Skype, Teams, or Zoom. Moreover, it increases the levels of interaction between the users in immersive virtual meetings. The users have an avatar that represents them and acts on their behalf. Therefore, virtual meetings are more similar to physical meetings than virtual meetings. This is why the meeting creates interfaces for the avatars in different forms that must be considered, and adjustments must be made according to the types of meetings.

Using hand tracking or the game controls described above allows users to pick up objects from the space and interact with them in front of the other players. Avatars can use their hands to touch each other and create physical communication by shaking hands, patting on the back, clapping, and more. In this section, the issue of privacy and personal spaces comes up in preliminary discussions to protect users' privacy.

Incidents of invasion of personal spaces and harassment may occur in virtual environments, and it is necessary to allow users essential tools to maintain their privacy. A small part of the options available on the platforms is a personal space that no other player can enter, or both participants' approval is needed to start creating a conversation and prevent random harassment and bullying.

With the help of the body movements and control of the avatar, the user can move around the infinite virtual spaces and perform actions such as walking, running, and even jumping and crawling. The body's movements are used to navigate the environment, but they are also partners in group transport and the realization of non-verbal communication between the users. Expressing emotions with the help of the body movements of the avatars allows a conversation that does not depend on language and is based on familiar movements such as happy dances, confirmation with hand gestures such as like, even expressions such as angry or ashamed and with an expression for most of the familiar emoji's.

Voice commands are the most familiar and straightforward tool for user interaction, enabling an open dialogue between the avatars. However, we want to maintain fundamental changes and establish a different language between the familiar conversation apps anad a virtual meeting. In that case, it is necessary to implement real-world physics so that if the user wants to have a private discussion with an avatar, he can access a private space with him, like a closed room, and be sure that we are in a private conversation and no one hears us. Another thing is the distance measurer. In the WEB 2.0 worlds, there are no distance differences between the users in the communication environment, so everyone hears everyone else with the same intensity and direction. Applying changes in sound intensities when moving away and getting closer between users intensifies the experience. It opens up possibilities of sensations from the real world so that if a user wants to reach a friend, he will have to physically approach and speak close to him or raise his voice to hear the others. The voice interactions change form and introduce tones of voice and non-monotonous conversation to which we have become accustomed in communication in the WEB 2.0 world. Social interaction in virtual worlds allows the creation of infinite situations that are all in the hands of the users. Positively and negatively, dispersing the players in the space according to groups, connecting avatars according to appearance, character traits, or topics of conversation. The principle of cooperation and teamwork can be well examined in how communities or individuals create social value in the space. As mentioned, how connections are made in the virtual spaces is more similar to the real world and practices skills that may have been lost to some users of WEB 2.0. In the virtual world, there is no ability to stand behind a keyboard and have an asynchronous and parallel conversation. The physical presence in the space does not allow it not to be connected to the living and active space. What happens in the virtual world is like a live broadcast. What users miss will not be repeated. Users cannot read previous messages or watch a replay. A discussion between the users happens once, and the avatar's presence is decisive and equivalent to a physical presence at an event such as an exhibition, a live performance, or a basketball or football game. Users who have experienced a virtual event use phrases like "I was there" since they perceive the event as an activity equivalent to being at the event in the physical world. The last element in user interaction is a multiplayer game element. The game is the essence of the virtual experience, and gamification is necessary for the virtual worlds to exist. The ability of players to make friends and communicate with other players through a game allows them to connect and break the ice immediately. The element of game competition offers a meeting place and a starting point for dialogue between the users, even the shy ones. The game itself brings the players of all genders and ends of the population to an equal meeting with more equal chances than in real life. The game lowers barriers of religion, race, and gender, as well as prejudices. Using gamification enables the globalization and distribution of ideas quickly and increases sociality in the virtual worlds.

3.1.2.3 INTERACTION WITH OBJECTS IN THE SPACE

This type of interaction allows users to control the environment around them. Considering the development of the virtual space, the assembly of the entire environment is a collection of objects that the creator must choose whether they can be disconnected from the environment and their interactive purpose. A piano placed in a virtual environment does not play by itself, and the creators have a central part of the experience in whether to allow the user to make use of the elements and how. The creators can allow realistic contact with the elements and give them physics and use as in the physical world. It is also possible to have an opposite experience or a combination of elements whose behavior in the virtual space contradicts how they operate in the physical world, thus intriguing and challenging the user.

The interaction with the elements is done through familiar body movements such as pulling, holding, pushing, swinging, and throwing.

When interacting, the user can receive haptic feedback from the environment to increase the immersion level and influence the activity's continuation. The haptic indication (see section 3.1.1) from the elements improves or impairs the user's performance and affects the selection of the following elements that the user chooses during the experience. Touching and using the elements is part of the user's orientation process in the environment to get to know it and the physics in which it exists. It is important to note that there are no identical environments. Getting to know the environment and the elements with which it is possible to interact will also affect the user's level of interaction in the space. The space's interaction process and physical abilities will increase if the user has prior familiarity. For example, in an environment with a target shooting game of arrows - a new user will examine in depth the table with the arrows, the manner of holding them, and their physical behavior compared to the familiar physical world, evaluating the weight of the arrows, the angle of the shot, the contribution of the power of the shot to the distance and how it is necessary to release the button to Let the arrow hit the target. All these parameters are determined by the platform's creators and are chosen according to the goals they set for themselves in creating the environment. There are no rules or protocols for these environments and no right or wrong. The user evaluates the quality of the platform while using it. If a user has had a positive experience, he will stay longer than a negative experience.

Familiarity with objects and the dimensions in which they appear in the environment allows the user a spatial understanding of the environment and increases their sense of presence. Training the rationale and connecting the user with familiar elements from the physical world help him get used to the space and give him a pleasant feeling of familiar spaces. However, there is no need to stick to familiar spaces since some of the virtual worlds' tools allow user experiences that cannot exist in the physical world. The correct dose of logic and breaking it will lead to success and an excellent experience for the user.

To conclude this part - breaking conventions in the way objects move can be the core of the experience, but breaking too many rules for the user can cause disorientation or a misunderstanding of the space, thus producing a negative experience and driving the users away due to an excess of desire to renew and change the familiar experiences.

3.1.2.4 INTERACTION WITH AI

The use of AI in virtual worlds can occur in several places and points of interaction between the user and AI. A natural language processing (NLP) interaction can occur when the user addresses a voice conversation to an avatar embodied by a computer or a natural conversation with the environment that responds to him. This method is conducted as a conversation in human-machine communication. It can reflect training situations in which an immediate response from the environment is needed. It can be to give feedback on an activity or help the user like a bot only more attractively and naturally in a conversation.

Machine learning to identify patterns and behaviors of the user can come into play when the user performs a series of moves or a particular move in a specific way. The machine can learn the user and adapt an automatic response that matches his patterns. So, for example, a person who often moves around the space quickly and is used to a fast pace of stimuli will be able to receive faster music, change elements in the space, and read tasks at a faster pace.

Interaction of the user with machine vision, the ability to integrate a camera that stands in front of the user and through it to create interactions with the environment, opens up unlimited possibilities for adding gestures and confirmations of the user. So, for example, it is possible to turn pages using a hand movement detected by an external camera or, for example, to allow an external camera to collect information about the user on the amount of time he enjoys during the experience (measured by facial features and smiles).

A simulation of a natural person's reaction through an avatar, referencing NPCs (Non- player characters) who react to every user movement by following the character or offering a particular object.

3.1.3 ILLUSTRATION

Developing an experience in virtual worlds will necessarily include simulation. If the simulation is photographed, there are more decisions related to the method and manner of photography, so I will not refer to this in the model. The tools available to content creators are from cinema and photography and do not enter into the models' parameters.

If so, creating content in virtual environments in a computerized way requires adherence to several parameters that will later affect other points in the model.

The thinking behind the introduction of development considerations in the illustration is that two key parameters can change decisions and direct projects toward success or failure depending on the needs.

3.1.3.1 SIMULATIONS OF INDOOR VERSUS OUTDOOR ENVIRONMENTS

Designing spaces is an art. The small details that make up the environment leave the first impression on the user, and the amount of information that passes to him by looking at the space is enormous. Looking in space at the details that have been invested can lead the viewer to conclusions even before starting the experience. He can make biased decisions due to prejudice or a wrong understanding of content. Building an outdoor environment requires much larger areas than indoor environments and, as such, requires more time for development, considering large spaces and thinking about the relationship of the objects to the user (for example, the height of trees or buildings near the user). The complexity of modeling the areas is understandable since it includes more items than interior environments and situations that must be considered, such as weather or the physics of vegetation in the space. The total number of variables in outdoor environments is greater and less controlled than indoor environments.

An interior environment is controlled and closed. An indoor environment will make it possible to ignore forces and physics in an open space, such as rain that wets certain areas or wind that moves leaves equally and logically to other vegetation in the area. In most cases does not include thinking to distort distant spaces or looking at the horizon, thereby eliminating the complexity of planning and execution and making the development process more manageable by thinking about the spaces and the physics of the weather conditions.

Outdoor environments are more interactive, with higher interactivity potential. For example, consideration must be given to the user's interaction with the environment when touching or exerting force on each of the objects and making decisions on the types of interactive objects. An example of more fantastic fun is what happens if the user walks around with a virtual gun in the forest and shoots trees. Will the ball show impact? Will it behave in the correct physics that a small tree will not repel the ball and a large tree will? Does the wind in the environment affect the accuracy of the shot?

Additional interactions to consider are the manner of movement in the space. Large spaces tend to adopt user running and jumping methods to shorten the user's idle time in the experience. In contrast, indoor environments will, by nature, be smaller, and the probability of interaction in space is lower. Control of physics in a closed environment is less sensitive to circulation in physics in open spaces.

3.1.3.2 GRAPHICS

Considering graphics, there are many creative methods for virtual worlds. The number of programs is relatively large, and the types of files can be different and will not necessarily allow switching between different programs. The choice of the graphic engine is crucial since the development process is complicated and complex, and it is not desirable, nor is it customary to switch between engines. Before choosing the engine, developers should comprehensively survey the graphics engines and choose the appropriate one.

High-poly and low-poly models refer to the number of polygons that comprise the assets. The assets are those parts that make up the complete visibility of the environment, including the accessories. Using low-poly will suit optimal performance and users with low-level end equipment. As of writing these lines, even high-level graphics engines aiming for realism in virtual reality still need to deal with high-poly satisfactorily. Although developers can see new versions of tools available in games or illustrations that are not VR, they will soon be available in VR. That means that on the development side, they will be able to reach a very high realistic level and, at the same time, provide good performance even on computers with relatively low specifications. It is important to note that the main reason for the burden of resources on the system is that game systems or "live" virtual environments are under the real-time category, and the calculation of the textures and the high amount of polygons are the ones that burden the system.

Scans of real-world props and environments are now performed by photogrammetry. They combine a large number of two-dimensional photographs to create a three- dimensional representation. These scans, in most cases, include much detail and burden the system resources. In order to implement it in virtual reality, it is necessary to ensure that the end-user has a high level of equipment and try to apply mathematical methods or methods from the development process to reduce the load on the system. One of the well-known methods is Level Streaming, in which the rendering process and extraction of system resources are carried out in parts of the environment and not the entire environment. Thus, with this method, it is possible to take a large environment that burdens the system's performance, cut it into parts, and present only parts of the environment to the user each time.

Realistic environments are characterized by decreased detail and visual reliability for the user and an experience of familiar visual elements. Some of the tools for creating credibility include referring to different light sources and realistic shading that considers the light's direction, intensity, and softening. A high and realistic level of graphics increases the level of immersion in the situation but simultaneously comes at the expense of computer performance.

On the other hand, caricaturistic environments at a low graphic level offer good performance to the point of renouncing computer processing and working on virtual reality glasses with an internal processor. However, of course, there are also concessions. Square areas with few curves characterize experiences of this type to reduce the number of polygons and optimize the content. The colors in this type of scene are uniform and do not include high-quality complex textures. They usually do not include shading and lighting images and always manage to achieve good performance at the expense of graphic quality.

There is no place here to determine whether one method is better. However, the correct way to look at the situation is to compare the requirements and what we are trying to achieve in the scene and determine the natural tendency for development following the data presented.

3.1.4 IMPACT

What is the ultimate goal of developing virtual environments, and what effect would we like to achieve? Why is this important? For each final goal, we would like to know the final impact on the environment and the user. By defining the goal and the impact, we can receive an indication of performance measurement at the end of the development of the experience. Has the development achieved its goals? We must categorize the types of influence and hence influence corresponding clauses to examine the degree of importance of each choice that will affect the final product.

3.1.4.1 IMPROVING THE USER EXPERIENCE

Compared to other physical or digital experiences, we have seen that the virtual worlds significantly impact the user. Using a different interactive experience in three- dimensional worlds improves the customer journey and the user experience, increasing engagement with the content. Hence, a memory of a unique experience in the customer motivates him to action.

3.1.4.2 REALISM-ORIENTED CONTENT TO CREATE A DIGITAL TWIN

Creating a real parallel world at its best emphasizes unique details, including high- quality textures, using technological tools to influence the senses, and using accessories for a controlled environment that resembles the real world as much as possible. Realistic capabilities aim to create a situation where the user will leave with a memory and a feeling of "I was there and experienced the situation" upon exiting the experience. The impression left on the user is a real memory that will affect him long- term. The skills and abilities he acquired during the experience are tools he can apply in the physical world if he encounters the situation. Therefore the value of acquiring knowledge, skills, and experience is extremely high.

3.1.4.3 STREAMLINE PROCESSES

This kind of effect is primarily an economic value and the correct utilization of resources. It is also possible to give up a human resource and replace it with a virtual one. Also, exchange of space resources or optimal utilization and independence in time and place. The virtual worlds can create situations that overcome gaps in the physical world that require investing many resources and optimizing processes, starting from simple work processes between teams in different parts of the world to the automatic management of a virtual factory that operates by avatars with artificial intelligence.

Furthermore, the virtual worlds can simulate situations that may happen in the physical world without actually creating them and save resources for creating complex environments, such as creating a deliberate fire in a forest or building and training firefighting forces. In these cases, beyond the direct saving of resources, there is the ability to train users to prevent indirect waste of resources, thus reducing the number of casualties, industrial wear and tear, waste of energy, time, and more.

3.1.4.4 INNOVATION

Many organizations these days have innovation departments or the position of an innovation leader. An organization's ability to touch and experiment with innovative tools puts the organization in the position of technological and innovative adoption. Organizations have a dual interest in being perceived as innovative. The first is so that the customers perceive the organization as innovative and thus contain a variety of positive perceptions about the organization (young, progressive, innovative products, etc.)—the second is so that the organization can experiment with various technologies. The idea of experimenting is to fail occasionally. No organization can contain all the technologies that exist in the market and adopt them. However, experimenting and failing is one of the methods to test the system and check whether the technology can meet the organization's needs. Since the technological worlds contain a variety of innovative technologies, there is a tendency in the innovation departments to go into pilots and experience the impact of the technology on the organization's employees. Furthermore, if it found a positive effect in one of the pilots, the organization will try to embark on another large-scale move and measure the return on investment.

3.1.4.5 MARKETING AND PUBLIC RELATIONS

Marketing activity is one of many issues in examining the effect. However, the effect surrounding the event is that organizations will want to establish their primacy and technological adoption when a new technology or idea enters the market. In most cases, this is a publicity stunt in which the organization carries out an activity with the help of technology and builds on the activity with a public relations system to appear in the various media and tell the story of how the organization uses technology. It does not matter what the actual effect the organization created with the help of technology. There is no internal organizational measurement in terms of return on investment. The move in advance created to invest in public relations rather than the technological use itself. In extreme cases, the implementation of the technology does not take place, or individual users use it only to provide images and videos for the publicity stunt. The risk is clear; the trick could harm the organization if discovered. The media coverage received in most cases is wide-ranging since it involves adopting innovative technology.

3.1.4.6 PURE ENTERTAINMENT

Humans love experiences and innovations. Furthermore, if we create innovation in how entertainment is consumed, we will potentially get a clientele that will want to experiment. The percentage of repeated use is irrelevant, although technology is a new and different experience for entertainment purposes. The range of physical experiences is extensive and includes, among other things: trips, bowling, entertainment complexes for the family, escape rooms, laser tag, skydiving or extreme sports, movie theaters, performing arts, and many more. Each of these experiences can be converted into a similar experience in virtual worlds, doubling the demand for the consumption of similar experiences.

To summarize this section, consideration must be given from the outset to the desired effect in the experience, thus adjusting the characteristics to the type of effect, allocating the resources to the elements needed to create the experience, thus creating a measure for examining the long-term and short-term impact of the activity.

3.1.5 IMPLEMENTATION

In implementing hardware in the field, there are many variables. No perfect product on the market meets all the requirements, so all the factors present in the devices must be examined. In addition, one must be familiar with the market and the hardware replacement frequency, and familiarity with future announcements can change the decision-making procedure to reflect the chosen virtual reality. Sometimes the newest is the best, and sometimes the newest suits the project. Also, in certain cases, there may be technologies that will discontinue. Therefore it is crucial to choose a type of technology that has long-term support. In monitoring technological development, it is recommended to get to know the companies in the market and follow firmware updates and sensor support that can help in the future with the project. When choosing the hardware, the customer's future needs must also be considered in the estimated product life span. In this section, we will divide the types of HMD and systems into several categories that indicate the type of helmet category and not a specific model. In each model, many variables must be taken into account: FOV (Field Of View), resolution, refresh rate, motion tracking method, comfort and organization, sound, compatibility with the corporate ecosystem, durability, price, user interface, accessibility to repair and spare parts, and more.

3.1.5.1 ENTRY LEVEL HMD

The cheapest and simplest augmented reality device is a cardboard smartphone holder. This holder makes use of the mobile device's screen as well as its gyro sensors and contains no technology. The device allows a wide distribution of a taste of the virtual world by viewing 360 content. This device provides functional limitations that do not allow it to provide a virtual reality experience.

One of the most significant limitations is the viewer's lack of interactivity with the content. The device is incompatible with gamepads, so only passive activity is possible. Beyond that, viewing quality determines the type of mobile phone users. For the most part, it enables viewing at a low resolution and a low screen refresh rate that damages the experience. Other limitations include limited usage time in the device's battery time, which should use as a daily tool as a phone, camera, and use of applications.

The movement restriction allows the user to experience movement in only three directions and to move the head. So movement in the space is impossible, and walking or moving during the experience will not affect the content. This limitation limits the user's possibilities to explore the virtual environment around him. Some opinions in the market support disqualifying this type of experience from being called "virtual reality".

This device is mainly used in institutions such as historical sites and museums, the field of education, and experiences representing a point of view for conveying a message of empathy or visiting a remote site. It will mainly be used for watching high-level filmed content or for basic experiences that allow the selection of questions or points of interest.

3.1.5.2 SCALING UP HMD

This family of devices is different. A primary device, which works with an internal operating system in the device, including lenses and display screens. A cheap device compared to the market, small in size, and has game controls. Users can use the HMD independently without a computer. This device also has a limit of free movement in space and allows viewing in three directions. The game controls, however, allow basic interaction with the content. Depending on the type of experience and other variables, glasses of this type will induce more nausea while using them. It will be difficult to implement interactive simulations or environments with high graphics that require high- level graphics card processing at such a device level.

Devices in the same price range also provide movement in 6 directions and are therefore unpopular. In most cases, the production of these devices discontinues. One of the severe limitations is the activation of the end customer's content. Several software solutions are designed to synchronize the helmets with content and remote control.

3.1.5.3 HYBRID HMD

Devices of this type stand by themselves and can process visual content with the help of monitors and processors in the device. They do not depend on external tracking sensors and do not require a computer. Also, devices of this type support the potential of using the 6 degrees of freedom of virtual reality and include game controls and sound from the device. Nothing is missing from it. However, one of the main limitations is graphic processing. Since the chips that operate devices of this type need to be more powerful, the users of these devices enjoy intermediate-level content and cannot break the graphics barrier for AAA content.

All AAA games require a computer connection to realize the potential of the content. The connection makes it possible to use the computer's graphics card, thus helping to break the graphic barrier of the helmet and enabling more complex interfaces with high graphic quality. It allows the hybrid platform to utilize the device's full potential with a cable connected to the computer, in some cases also through a wireless connection.

Whether connected to a computer or not, tracking sensors for location detection are embedded in the HMD. In most of the new advanced devices, there are also eye-tracking sensors and even lip readers. These devices bring out the best when mobility and independence from a computer are required. On the other hand, they realize their full potential with a connection to a computer.

3.1.5.4 PCVR HMD

PCVR HMD devices are virtual reality glasses connected to a computer containing a high-level graphics processor. Most devices offer rich technical specifications and advanced capabilities. The most advanced devices contain eye tracking sensors, high resolution, wide viewing angle, hand tracking, and even pass-through viewing (through the cameras) to see the environment. Different types of companies develop tracking of the user's movement; some use the device's cameras to perform the tracking, and some use a more accurate tracking method with what is called Lighthouse. In some devices, users can add tracking sensors and connect them to additional objects, whether limbs, to create full-body tracking or connecting to objects to create synchronization between physical objects and the virtual world. The collection of body movement data is so precise that it is possible to use them to analyze movement in sports or the world of rehabilitation.

The field of science, research, design, and heavy industry fields need accurate tools to simulate realistic worlds or be accurate in data collection. In most cases, they will use high-level devices over hybrid devices.

3.1.5.5 HIGH-END HMD

The highest quality HMD on the market can be found today in the VARJO company, which produces virtual reality glasses with a high standard that focuses on the quality of the material, high resolution for viewing precise details and reading texts in virtual worlds, as well as distinguishing fine textures, which is essential in the fields of design, engineering, archeology, and art. The advanced eye tracking technology allows tracking the exact area where the user is watching and thus investing computer resources only in the relevant parts instead of creating a load on the computer in processing the entire environment. The wide viewing angle of 115 degrees allows the user to make fewer unnecessary head movements and concentrate on the experience, increasing immersion. The HMD type is among the few that supports two tracking methods, both with and without external sensors. By considering these five factors (3.1.1-3.1.5), businesses can gain a more comprehensive understanding of their digital transformation agenda and make informed decisions about how to proceed. This model clarifies the process and reduces the risk of failure, enabling businesses to build more successful and impactful virtual worlds.

3.2 THE SOLUTION- INVERSE BUILDER

This section will present a comprehensive solution for successful digital transformation in businesses. This solution is designed to help organizations overcome the challenges of digital transformation and leverage the full potential of new technologies such as the VR metaverse. I will explore the critical components of this solution, including the infrastructure required to support digital transformation, the user interfaces necessary to deliver engaging experiences, and the data analytics capabilities required to gain insights and make informed decisions. I aim to simplify the digital transformation process and help businesses achieve their digital transformation goals by providing organizations with an integrated solution that addresses all of these critical components.

3.2.1 INTRODUCTION

With the release of the first website in 1991, a real revolution began that affected our lives from end to end. The world has changed - the nature of human consumption, the ability to search for information, the learning tools and skills, the language required to navigate the world, new professions, interpersonal interaction, and many more.

The Internet brought with it a fundamental change of perception. Since all services are transferred to digital, the average person must have a basic digital orientation to consume services, whether typing and moving the mouse or filling out online forms and sending an email. Knowing this primary language produced standardization in the consumption of information. Later, file types such as JPG and PDF or sending ZIP files entered the lexicon, and it was clear to users of online platforms. When the word website was said, everyone knew how to type WWW.

Now the next stage of the Internet has reached our lives. We see the same signs of a lack of digital orientation in operating new devices, a lack of standardization, and learning a different language than typing and using a mouse. In such early stages, it is advisable to prepare the ground and create accessible bridges. Accessibility can take all forms, and there is no dominant method. One of the ways is to make use of an existing orientation in order to create content and knowledge in the technology of the future. In the early stages of any technology, there is a need for deep and inaccessible knowledge about how the technology works and, in addition, knowledge of programming to implement it. Users are often reluctant to try new things. To help users, developing a platform as simple as possible and expandable as the digital orientation process progresses is necessary. For example, websites were written in code before accessible platforms such as WIX, SHOPIFY, and SQUARE SPACE entered our lives, which presented a no-code platform for creating websites. As of today, there are almost 2 Billion websites that point to the potential of new no-code platforms for the digital world.

3.2.2 INVERSE NO-CODE VERSITES BUILDER

No-code platforms allow the average user to produce with the help of accessible tools without prior programming knowledge to implement a complete and active product.

Platforms of this type present a convenient interface in terms of visibility and functionality, including explanations and tips on creating a primary product and more in-depth explanations for changing advanced functionality. The accepted method is usually the familiar drag and drop using the mouse. Sometimes, it is possible to load a template with the click of a button and start from a more advanced stage.

Dragging objects on the platform is convenient for the user functionally and in the user interface. Behind each object is a code with functionality that can be adjusted. When selecting the object, a menu allows users to enter numbers or drag a bar from right to left to control the parameters. The idea of the platform is to provide tools and not content and, therefore, offers as many options and functionality as possible to suit different target audiences. All platforms, without exception, start with a basic interface and upgrade the functionality over time.

No-code platforms contain many advantages, mainly in accessibility to unskilled or low-budget target audiences. With a low budget of tens of dollars per month, they allow the production of an active product to be done quickly. The monthly cost of using such a platform is equivalent to the price of a programmer's hour in most cases. Another
advantage is that the no-code platforms are easy to use. Pulling objects allows the user to see immediate results. The required orientation is fundamental; any basic computer user can experiment with it. The platforms' use is very flexible, allows adjustments according to the customer's needs, and usually contains adjustments according to relevant business types or niches. Moreover, the platforms make it possible to realize the concept of an idea into a prototype within a day.

A no-code platform for virtual worlds completely differs from a no-code platform for websites.

Interface: Websites displayed in two dimensions allow using elements such as buttons, sliders, links, and opening and enlarging images. The tools are known in the two- dimensional world to change shape and enable content from any direction. Virtual worlds are 3D and, as such, enable a complex interactive experience. Building in 3D may be complex for some users since it requires spatial perception and an understanding of gamification. In no-code platforms for virtual worlds, it is necessary to animate objects, and the possible settings are multiplied several times compared to websites. Thinking about immersive content in 360 is a complex skill that has not yet been cracked, and many methods allow for endless creativity.

User Interactions: Websites do not exist in a live multi-user world, and interaction does not happen in real-time. There is a delay in user responses, and the interaction is mainly written or spoken. Therefore, the platform builders must allow various interactions that include game diversity and provide rewards. In the virtual worlds, the interactive experience with objects is the most significant, and it is the one that will keep the users longer in the virtual world. This wide world can explore additional tools to continue the interactions outside the virtual world to create continuity and a point of attraction to return and use virtual worlds.

Development tools: the websites allow familiar capabilities of elements for writing, talkback, chat options, uploading images, etc. The programming languages, website development languages, and the rules for the consumer are pretty fixed. In the development of 3D experiences, new worlds without standards are revealed. There is no uniformity in the development tools. The interactions are not yet mature, the menus' interfaces and user interactions are still in development, and the user's equipment is still under development at a high frequency. Therefore, new interfaces come out every few weeks and disrupt the development and support of the devices. The style of interactions changes daily due to hand tracking and multiple controls with different buttons. There are many file formats and no smooth transition between the different 3D software. Creating a development pipeline lasts only briefly and should be changed frequently. Developments for 3D experiences require API interfaces and multiple uses of SDKs that require a large number of talents in the team to develop an immersive experience that includes, among others, DevOps, animators, character designers, storytellers, element designers, environment designers, real-time optimization experts, And other crew members who are more like a studio production crew than a one-man show.

Outcomes:

Websites are products accessible through browsers on various devices such as laptops and desktops, cell phones, tablets, and supporting televisions. The development tools enable automatic adjustment of the site's dimensions to the device's size, and there is no need for manual adjustment to the consumer's device but to the browser.

Virtual experiences are accessible from various devices, including computers and immersive devices such as VR glasses. These require many adjustments to support many types of HMD and different operating systems and drivers.

The platform I chose to develop with the development team tries to trace all the digital gaps mentioned in the previous chapters and decipher solutions to the difficulties arising from the different development styles concerning the web. The platform bridges the skills required in the virtual worlds. The drag-and-drop tool in a two-dimensional interface is familiar and enables a pleasant connection with potential customers. The development team researched and worked according to the 5 i's model and designed the platform to yield the maximum possible to meet most of the user's needs without needing to know the model himself. The platform was built with advanced thinking to make it easier for the consumer and remove complex barriers from his responsibility, such as matching the graphic level to most average computers or supporting both computers and virtual reality glasses. This reduced user objections to experimenting with the platform. The platform is a collection of main features from over

100 projects for different industries. Some features are at the design and user interface level, some at optimizing the graphics, and some at building clean code and fast running without bugs and crashes. The platform was developed to an operational prototype level with active users for two years, from March 2021 to March 2023, and is still developing with the addition of new customers.

3.2.3 INVERSE BUILDER DESCRIPTION

INVERSE is a revolutionary no-code VR metaverse builder that is incredibly user-friendly and intuitive. It empowers businesses to create their virtual world effortlessly and embark on a digital transformation journey. The essential part of INVERSE's software is its drag-and-drop interface that allows users to easily design and customize their virtual environment without requiring programming skills. With INVERSE, users can easily create interactive 3D experiences, integrate multimedia content, and host virtual events. This section describes in detail the development behind the software.

3.2.3.1 INFRASTRUCTURE

Product infrastructures are one of the most critical things in assembling the puzzle. Building a shaky infrastructure could collapse the entire house of cards. On the other hand, it is impossible to anticipate all the changes along the way, so we had to think about versatile work that will allow a certain flexibility during the development. For the benefit of the project, we worked and experimented with all three primary cloud services, including Google's GCP, Microsoft's AZURE, and Amazon's AWS. All three services provided a good result. The most prominent AZURE provided easy access to additional interfaces we needed further down the road, such as a mobile gaming support service. In addition, at the beginning of 2023, it announced it would allow connection to artificial intelligence models. The maximum number of users in each environment depends on several factors, some under control and some not. What we have control over is the hardware required in the cloud, which can theoretically support hundreds of users simultaneously. Our software is developing on the infrastructure of EPIC, the subsidiary of UNREAL - the development engine. The limit on the number of users comes from EPIC's decision and development. After carrying out load tests, the virtual worlds we built can reach and contain the maximum number of approved players on existing EPIC systems. When connecting to the platform, we recommend connecting wired and not via WIFI, which may reduce stability and cause local user crashes. We found creative solutions. Even if the meeting host runs into a technological challenge, the other users continue the session, and the host reconnects to the experience. In building games and experiences, there is value in the delay in the time of interactions between the players. To get short response times that would be of high quality and relevant to users, we tested servers almost anywhere in the world and at different connection rates until we arrived at the perfect recipe that detects the user's connection location and directs them to servers with low ping for an optimal experience.

3.2.3.2 BUILD INTERFACE

The development of the build interface took a long time. The adjustments in the interface were complex since it was necessary to flatten the entire 3D world and, at the same time, allow the versatility of the 3D. The solution was to assemble environments from a view, then change the angle of each wall and view it two-dimensional on both sides. To understand spatial perception and the distance between the objects, we added a 3D preview button where builders could move around the virtual environment. The interface is structured as one page on the right side, with subject categories for chairs, tables, and decoration. Clicking on one of the categories opens the window, and the objects are displayed and ready to be dragged to the left side, where the work canvas appears with accurate distance axes for the size of the environment.

In the build interface, a user can add materials and ready content from the 2D worlds, such as graphics, photos, and videos, that builders can integrate into the 3D worlds. Each environment can be saved locally and uploaded to the cloud in real time. In addition to helping the user build environments, we added environment templates familiar to users following previous projects, including galleries, sales halls, showrooms, interactive escape rooms, training rooms, lectures and conferences, and more. To integrate live performances or live lectures, we added a live stream feature in a simple way to common platforms such as Zoom and Facebook. To strengthen the relationship with the potential customers and create engagement, We added elements such as taking digital photos and sending them as souvenirs. In addition, we added links to products to receive extended information in the email address about products and purchase options.

3.2.3.3 USER INTERFACE

The user interface was first developed with a vision of accessibility. The ability to make the system accessible to the user will be similar to his skills and allow him to stay in the system and experiment. We removed The registration process, and the user can connect to the system only by entering a name that will be displayed. Also, it is not mandatory to enter an email. In the long term, there is a goal to carry out some registration process, and it may be possible to register with one click through Google details or any other system. It was crucial to us to allow the customer to download only one software and not to confuse him with a few installations. Therefore, we had to separate from the servers of the STEAM company and allow customers a transparent system when we used EPIC's parallel systems in the background.

The choice of avatar allows for a variety of generic characters divided equally between men and women. To make it easier for the user to choose the environment, he can tap on the name of an area that contains several environments, and only those will be visible. This will allow easy access to desired areas. Access to the environments will be possible simultaneously on a computer and virtual reality devices. The software recognizes the type of device and hence provides the user with a different menu depending on the type of device, thus enabling a familiar interface. Also, when interacting with items in the space or with other people, the appearance of the interactions is adjusted according to the device to maximize comfort. Since the technology does not yet allow sufficient levels of avatar mimics, we have added to the interaction system an emotion wheel where users can choose an emoji that indicates their mood, and the avatar behaves accordingly. Sharing feelings is an essential tool in the interaction between users and conveying the nature of the message, which sometimes could go better in writing or sound without body language. At each stage of the experience, when approaching interactive objects, there is guidance on which buttons to use to make it easier for the user to remember all the buttons. Even when using virtual reality glasses, it is difficult to stop the experience in the middle and check the key settings. Overall, the user interface makes it easier for the user in every possible way to provide him with a pleasant and easy initial experience and to allow the user to later choose more complex options from the basic experience. The importance of accessibility is ensuring the customer is satisfied and feels comfortable staying around for a long time.

3.2.3.4 LOGS AND INRERACTION DATA COLLECTION

The data collection system is not to collect data about the user as is customary in the web world for advertising purposes. The main goal in collecting the interaction data is to allow the builders of the environments to receive reliable information about the quality of the environment. Another possibility is the ability to evaluate the individual user when performing tasks in groups with other users and create menus and information relevant to the user to improve the quality of the experience for him. The database collects the following data: the names of the users who entered the experience and the time they spent there, the period in which there was a load of users, the amount of interactions between users, the interaction times of a user with objects in the environment, on the object side it is possible to know how long all users interacted with the object and the level of popularity relative to others. At this stage, the information is stored on servers, the insights are extracted manually from tables, and there is no accessible dashboard for the environment builders. In this initial phase, we performed several tests to integrate artificial intelligence systems, mainly in language analysis. It will make it possible to evaluate each user's contribution, rate him, and extract meaningful information from the speech in the experience. The AI tools are only used with the user's permission since a microphone records what is happening in the environment. The information obtained from the language analysis is very diverse. It includes, among other things, speech speed data, use of leading words, word count, use of optimistic versus pessimistic language, and more. The data collection system is still in its initial stages as there is still a regulatory road to go through to use the data wisely. Later on, it will be possible to collect biometric data with the help of various sensors mounted on virtual reality helmets. Collecting biometric data raises many moral questions that must be characterized, and the uses of biometric data must be considered before they are collected. It also ensures the security of the data since biometric data is difficult to change, if at all.

3.3 CASE STUDY RESULTS

Proper implementation of the model and use of the software will yield positive results from the digital transformation process. In order to validate the assumption, I present a case study and analyze it in all its stages, from thinking about the solution to implementation in the field. The analysis of the case is based on the proposed model and its application with the help of INVERSE software. The analysis will include a background on the project's requirements, an in-depth analysis of the model in the context of a specific project, the analysis of the research data I performed, and a summary of its result.

3.3.1 BACKGROUND

Training officers and guards are part of their work routine. Training refreshes guidelines, updates procedures, and trains the security forces to better prepare for real-time incidents. Field exercises are done regularly to practice cases and responses. An incorrect response or incompetence in managing crises can cost human lives. In particular, law enforcement and correctional officers usually train using traditional methods that include classroom study and role plays between the learners. The effect of the learning process on the security of the prison and the prisoners is essential. At the beginning of 2020, the world experienced a terrible outbreak of Covid-19, and many activities were stopped, including flights, events, studies, exhibitions, entertainment shows, and more. As a result, there was significant difficulty in carrying out training that included contact between participants. The trainees were also prevented from traveling between areas to receive the training. The state of prisons in the whole world was even more problematic since, in prison, it is more difficult to maintain social distancing and manage hygiene. In our case, before the outbreak of the virus, officers and guards would fly from all over Europe to perform training in different locations in real prisons to perform simulations in the physical prison cells.

This process was in addition to traditional learning and learning in online courses and tests. The physical training procedure was an applied part for which the organization required to fly trainees from different places, accommodations, and lodgings, as well as many training teams, a production team to arrange and organize the situation, assessment teams, and other additional resources. As part of the HORIZON 2020 grant program, I participated as a team member in developing a solution for training correctional officers in program number 763714 called JSAFE, Judicial Strategy Against all Forms of Violent Extremism in Prison.

Before the coronavirus outbreak, we developed local training for a single player using virtual reality glasses. The trainee searched for prohibited objects in a generic prison cell. At the end of the software development and just before the implementation in the field, all the flights were canceled, and so was the training, thus making the development irrelevant to the training program. The development team returned to the table for brainstorming and developed lesson plans and training in the metaverse (multiplayer) experiences. The training is based on the exact original requirement that will allow law enforcement teams the opportunity to train. The process took about a year and a half, from the development to the implementation, including the data collection to carry out impact research.

The test case will review the digital transformation process, starting from the thinking process to the implementation in the field. It analyzes according to the proposed 5 i's model (section 3.1). The case study focuses on solving the problem of accessibility to law enforcement training in an era of restrictions and social distancing. The problem statement is improving prison officer training by providing a more realistic and practical environment.

The case study will examine the quality of training for a carefully selected focus group and suggest improvement and preservation processes for additional projects.

3.3.2 SOLUTION- 5 I'S MODEL ANALYSIS

Before proposing the solution for implementing virtual reality systems that include multiple participants in the European Union project, a think tank was assembled. The team included a development manager, 3D modelers, an animator, a defense product manager, researchers from the academy, a training officer on behalf of the European Union, training officers from the prison in Padua (in Italy), and a technical person specializing in virtual reality. The team analyzed the project according to the 5 i's model and submitted product requirements documents for approval. Here is the analysis of the model and the considerations taken in the successful project:

3.3.2.1 IMMERSION

First, we tried to understand the level of digital orientation of the teams intended to use the software. We came to understand that these are mainly teams aged 45 and over.
Most have never used virtual reality, did not wear an HMD, learned in traditional ways, and primarily used web browsers. The input of the technical people in the team was that people new to the virtual worlds would have difficulty grasping several technologies simultaneously, and one should try to minimize the new technological accessories when implementing the solution. The prison training officers demanded that the experiences be as realistic as possible and asked to increase the immersive level of the content with the help of wearable accessories. The development team proposed, for the first phase of the project, a significant investment in the architectural precision of the content to simulate the actual prison cells, which included the design of the prison structure according to photos and also exact measurements of the size of the cells, the toilets, the windows, the prisoners' beds, and the storage cabinets. Also, the development team

requested photos of the design of all the other rooms of the prison director, the clinic, the meeting room, and the prison yard to illustrate the accuracy of the details. We recorded The small details in the list of requirements down to the minor details of the security arrangements at the place, the location of cameras, and the distance between the bars. In the first phase, no additional wearable accessories were added to the users. Moreover, attempts were made in the laboratory to produce real bulletless guns consisting of airsoft guns with recoil gas; these were connected to micro switches inside the gun used as a game controller. Instead of firing a real weapon, the trainees could hold a dummy weapon and feel natural recoil. A preliminary attempt to create a gun to increase immersion resulted in the fact that in a small group of experimenters, we could understand that it was indeed correct not to integrate additional tools other than a virtual reality system. Connecting additional accessories was too early.

We decided on a preliminary orientation phase for the experience in which all the trainees will go through a session to learn the remote control buttons in virtual reality. After that, the system will test them for about 5 minutes to see whether they get along with the buttons and know the new technological tool. This step will avoid technical malfunctions resulting from unfamiliarity with the device. Thus, we will increase the level of connection between the trainees and the content and create a more immersive experience.

3.3.2.2 INTERACTION

The four types of interaction came to the discussion table, and thus, we tried to offer the correct ways to produce an accurate and intuitive interaction for the user. There were several ways to perform each type of interaction. Each team member experimented with the type of interaction to experience it practically and then gave feedback from his field of expertise.

Interaction with menus - this type of interaction is not yet uniform in any virtual reality experience, nor is there a standard in the industry. It took much work to determine how to open menus, tap the selection buttons, and change user settings. In order to make it easier for the average user, most options were left to the professional guide who joined the experience and accompanied the trainees. The guide had more capabilities with complex menus to change settings, change content worlds, lead players, and run games within the experience. The menu was personal and hidden from the other players to avoid disturbing them during the experience. Each participant could choose the language of the experience for their native language and not English as the accepted default. In the development phase at those times, hand-tracking technology was still immature. Although using hand gestures is more intuitive than controllers, a lack of multi-functionality led the development team to offer the use of controllers but to facilitate the user with a single selection button that included a virtual laser beam that indicates the location of the selection. The menu has been pre-prepared with very large buttons to make it easier for users to aim with high precision if they have difficulty. The menu was simple in a gray color palette, and when the laser pointed to a specific area, the button was highlighted in vivid colors to highlight the selection.

We removed Buttons indicating the start or exit of the experience from the menu. The choice to start or end the experience was up to the guide. This way, we created the experience for the user so that he would not be required to use the menu regularly during the experience and thus remove a barrier in the orientation process. When choosing the button that opens the menu, we chose a button that is not naturally accessible on the game controller, thus preventing the menu from opening unintentionally since new users tend to press many buttons and get confused between them.

Interaction with artificial intelligence - In this project, artificial intelligence was used sparingly. Some of the reasons were budget and time constraints for the project.

However, we built the system so that its base would be ready to implement artificial intelligence in avatars and data analysis. However, we implement creative ways to create a feeling that avatars simulating the prisoners are not statues or dolls and can have a basic interaction according to a behavior tree we built for them in advance. For example, if a prisoner must give a password to a mobile phone caught in the prison cell, he can randomly cooperate or resist.

Interaction with objects - in this experience, we implemented over 200 objects in different interaction groups. Some objects cannot be moved, some are limited to moving a part of the object (like a storage cabinet door), some can be fully moved, and some can be opened and disassembled. In addition, a unique group of objects is complex objects with a purpose and use, such as a metal detector, when interacting with other objects. For each object, we had to define the level of its use and what it affects in the scene. During the accuracy of the details, many questions arise about each object. What happens if it falls from the grip of the hand? Is it disposable? Will placing the object in the right place make it disappear or earn the user a point? Can others in the scene see all the objects and each other's interactions with the object?

There were many more questions, but the development team made decisions that simplified the user's interaction and reduced complex interactions. For example, if an object falls from the hand, it returns to its original place, so the user does not have to bend down and try to pick up objects that sometimes get stuck in complex areas.

While running a situation simulation, we tried to make it easier for the user to use the one and only button to interact with objects. While there is no physical contact between the avatar and the object, the user's hand becomes a "like" sign, and when there is contact between objects and the user, the hand becomes a functioning hand and can pick things up, rotate, and pass them on. In cases where it was necessary to place objects in different locations, we helped them with the SNAP system that attaches the object to its correct location. That is because the trainees tested on the methodical successes in the content rather than on their digital orientation.

Interaction with other players - First, we created a naming system to identify other players. The name appears regularly above the avatar. Using the name of an existing avatar in the experience is impossible. The communication between the players is mainly through speech. When the behavior of the sound in the space corresponds to reality, as users move away from each other, the intensity of the sound fades. Also, moving to another room with a door or a dividing wall will block the sound, and one player cannot hear the other players. Some interactions have been removed to comply with GDPR privacy standards. In one of the attempts, we presented a practical example and asked some guides for photos to create avatars for them. Due to privacy standards, the European Union rejected the idea, and we removed the avatars. We had to make use of several generic male and female characters. To maintain a private space, we added a radius of one meter that cannot be entered and is the personal space. The users could transfer objects to each other to produce joint work to complete the tasks. Although we have the technology to implement a full-body recognition algorithm, it was decided to leave generic characters without motion tracking, remove the entire waist area, and flatten the characters to avoid situations of dealing with body images irrelevant to the activity. To prevent unintentional interruption of activity in advance, avatars cannot affect the body image of other avatars. In the event of an unexpected collision, the avatars pass through each other. This mode also allows for a workload in a crowded area like a prison cell to produce many interactions without interruption.

3.3.2.3 ILLUSTRATION

We received some of the requirements in advance when we approached the project. Most of the requirements covered a lot of the confusion for us when the subject of illustration came up. To simulate virtual reality, we eliminated the possibility of scanning the areas. The scans result in high detail accuracy (high-poly) that does not allow for processing on average computers. Moreover, we did not have the physical possibility since the flights were canceled, and we called to solve the accessibility problem to the training area. The demand was to produce an environment parallel to the real world, called a digital twin. To complete the task, we asked for drawings and measurements of all the items and areas as accurately as possible and original photos from the same place, including indoor and outdoor environments. We reviewed all the existing walls and surfaces and tried to indicate what they were made of. That allowed us to add unique textures to create a realistic experience. Some of the textures consisted of rubbed concrete, peeling walls, scraped irons, rust residues, and different types of glass. How the textures were adapted to the accessories produced a realistic simulation at a significant level. In our case, the outdoor environments were more straightforward to measure than classic outdoor environments since they were enclosed by the prison walls, which allowed us to ignore the modeling of the horizon line and many details in the space. In videos we got from the place, we generated knowledge about the nature of the vegetation that grew between the prison walls and created green areas, according to the videos. According to the weather that season, we created light gusts of wind to revive the situation that the vegetation would move a little and raise the illusion of a living environment. The subject of the prisoners was challenging. We got information from the officers about the prisoners' character to create diversity in the avatars without harming a particular population. We also asked to receive information about their clothing type and how they interact in the green and sports yards.

From the videos we received, we simulated groups of prisoners talking.

We created the characters with clear facial features at a realistic level and not a low level of graphics.

We have created several random movements for all the characters that will move in space or talk with their hands to create the realistic feeling of a living and breathing environment. In creating the environments and the graphic level, we also had to consider the budgets for the equipment purchase since purchasing more expensive equipment would have allowed the use of a higher graphic level. We also adapted the graphic level to how the chosen virtual reality system works. We could work knowing that the virtual reality system is connected to a computer with a graphics processor and does not work based on a chip embedded in glasses without a computer. This option allowed us to make many visual adjustments to a realistic level. Throughout the development time, we had to perform optimization tests for several video cards and ensure that we stayed within the graphics capabilities of the processors.

3.3.2.4 IMPACT

The impact was clear to all team members. The goal of the project was to bring success to the training. However, the think tank came up with several ways to generate significant additional values to generate additional impact. We made economic calculations on how much money was saved by switching to a virtual reality activity without arriving at the training camp. The exact number cannot be published, and several interpretations of what is included under the savings clauses exist. However, it is about saving millions of dollars in staff, flights, and accommodation—additional savings value due to the impact of streamlining processes. Before performing the activity in virtual reality, the training was conducted in small groups, and the waiting time for the experiment could have been hours. Also, arranging the cells for the next group took time. Thus, the trainees also lost attention and concentration and performed less well.

Conducting the training in virtual reality means that it is now possible to create an infinite replication of the number of sites where training can be provided. The amount depends on the number of VR stations the organization purchases.

3.3.2.5 IMPLEMENTATION

The process of planning the application and deciding on the type of HMD required the team to consider the mandatory clauses in the European Union requirement to develop the experience. After analyzing all types of HMD, we removed the option of stand-alone glasses. There are two main reasons for this. The first is the need to carry out the training together, collect data, and rely on dedicated servers in the cloud. A second reason is the high-level graphics and creating an experience as close to reality as possible. To enable experience and interaction with the content, we had to reject glasses that do not support movement in all directions (6DOF). We also ruled out the highest level of VR because of the technology costs and the huge space they require.

We left with a choice of high-quality helmets that support walking in space. We can connect them to a high-end computer and use the video cards to utilize their potential fully. Plan how we will perform the installation. We decided that a local team in the destination country would order the HMD and the computer according to the company's instructions, after which a technical person would take over the computer and perform adjustments and driver updates. After that, several more users connect and do load tests. From experience in previous projects like this, it is possible to more easily control the virtual reality glasses and the computer, thus assisting in remote control when necessary. In the type of glasses we tested, physical objects can be connected with sensors that indicate the location of the objects in space. This allowed us to experiment with embedding guns and advanced training. In addition, the advanced type of glasses received frequent software updates and included support for future eye and hand tracking with the potential to upgrade the project. Also, accessibility to purchase equipment in the target countries was critical since it is impossible to obtain equipment in every European country. Before the start of the development, we made sure that local suppliers had stock and the ability to supply the customers with the computers and HMDs.

3.3.3 THE ITALIAN CASE-RESULTS AND CONCLUSION

We chose Italy as a case study due to the ability to train five professional instructors to deliver the training to the other prison officers. A technical representative was present in the field who was trained in advance to train instructors and thus allow the officers to examine and evaluate their co-workers. The virtual reality experience developed for the training was based on the analysis process of the 5 i's model, and the basis of the experience was developed using the INVERSE non-code platform. It must be qualified and said that the system in those days was not accessible to the end consumer, and the development team used it to shorten development times. Today the system is accessible for use by end consumers.

The focus group included 36 experimenters who were all in the age range of 45-55. This age group has in common that 100% of the participants served as senior officers for over 20 years. In all the previous years, the officers were trained in traditional and digital ways. In training for the security forces, they have a source of comparison to evaluate the learning process in virtual reality objectively. Another thing the group has in common is that everyone has never tried virtual reality before. To neutralize the advantage that may exist for those who have already experienced both digital orientation and the strength of the impact and the first impression.

First, everyone went through an individual experience that gave them a basic digital orientation to use the device. Due to the nature of the job and the gender distribution in the organization, two-thirds were men, and the rest were women.

We divided the training into chapters where, in total, each experimenter spent about two hours in an experiential learning process in virtual reality. At the end of the experience, we talked with all the experimenters about their impressions of the process to test its effectiveness, which, as mentioned, was developed with the help of the two primary tools mentioned in this study.

From all experimenters, 76% of them reported that training using Metaverse in virtual reality was more beneficial than traditional methods. In the whole process, one experimenter refused to participate and claimed that this training method was not suitable for his age and that he assumed that younger people would be able to connect with the concept. In addition, 2 (about 5%) experimenters who went through the experience claimed it was ineffective. Although we performed preliminary preparation and digital orientation, only 60% of the experimenters claimed the technology was simple. However, despite the difficulty and sometimes also the dissatisfaction, 100% of the experimenters praised the quality of the content and the methodical development and felt they could connect with the visual content. Also, all the experimenters, without exception, felt more comfortable being with the trainer during the virtual experience. It was effective and necessary.

At the end of the discussion, we asked trainees to indicate verbally honestly what experiences from virtual reality training would describe the experience. Among the sentences: "major engagement," "living scenarios that otherwise would be impossible to try," and "first-hand experience."

Some trainees confirmed that learning by doing leaves a more significant mark, and the memory and content remain in memory and influence the learning process.

Despite the small number of participants, I see the process and its results as a significant success for the relevance of implementing the model and using the INVERSE platform to influence the training segment, improve results and save resources.

4. SUMMARY

In the conclusion of this thesis, I will present the research proposal's conclusions that answer the research question. I will present the limitations and caveats that must be considered in implementing the model and guidance. I will develop thinking ideas for the future and ideas for further research. I will introduce the subject of artificial intelligence, which is an integral part of the virtual worlds, and integrate it into subsequent studies.

4.1 SUMMARY AND CONCLUSION

The problems and challenges facing the metaverse industry, particularly virtual reality, were presented to conclude this applied research. Acknowledging the challenges and recognizing the corresponding period at the beginning of the Internet era are ways to recognize and offer a solution to the digital transformation from WEB 2.0 to WEB 3.0. The logic leading this work is to use methods and solutions that have worked in the past and make adjustments to the existing technology. In the literature, as we saw in the review, there are islands of success in niche research explaining the effects of puzzle pieces. The research offers a broad perspective on solving macro business problems and dealing with changing processes and concepts. This applied research brings innovation to the world of research and offers an established and up-to-date model at the time of writing this research. The model enables business analysis of think tanks before embarking on large-scale projects. The model aims to minimize the damage that may have been caused by the failure of the digital transformation process. The analysis outline covers most of the weak points for possible failure and thus may increase the percentage of success. The model focuses on one method among the most effective:

Metaverse using virtual reality. The no-code platform makes it possible to bridge all the mentioned digital gaps for small-medium businesses that want to make a digital transformation to the virtual worlds but cannot invest the enterprise's resources.

The applied research analyzed the interactions and infrastructures needed to implement digital transformation. Now businesses are not required to invest resources and implement an easily accessible transformation. It must be remembered that there are other methods to adopt virtual worlds and carry out digital transformation. The two applied products in this work exist side by side but do not require parallel applications of both together. Businesses can use the 5 i's model and implement a process that uses other platforms or processes, including code development. It is also possible to use the INVERSE platform without the model since it was developed based on the principles of the model and meets the needs of businesses on most points. I offer the model as an open model that can add and subtract sections from it according to technological progress. Part of building a technological model is allowing it to exist in a developing and changing environment; therefore, it is correct for its time and for the technological context to which it refers.

4.2 LIMITATION

I wrote this applied research out of my belief that there have been many changes in the field while developing and researching this work. Many investments by large companies in the industry went down the drain, and projects by companies like Meta and Microsoft were closed and left a bad taste. In addition, the number of investments in the markets decreased drastically, and many startups in the industry closed. On the other hand, according to Gartner's technology hype cycle, this is a natural process of technology, and the productivity phase is getting closer. In the limitations of the research, there may be other elements that I didn't cover, including information security and cyber-attacks, identity theft, and the development of a new generation of hackers. Also, within the limitations of the study, it should be remembered that the author of the study is a partner in a company with limited resources, and active companies in the economy that have raised millions of dollars may offer equally good platforms from a technological point of view and adjustment possibilities. In the case study, I analyzed the field of law enforcement forces. Limitations detailing many cases, including the cases in which the digital transformation process failed. Lessons learned from it and the platform includes them without detailing the failure case studies.

In many cases, the assimilation process is minimal, and the doors to researching the implementation process are closed for us. Companies do not want to disclose and present results or are afraid of the data collected about them. Apart from the numerical data, part of the assimilation and accompaniment process is also important, preventing the implementation teams from passing on information about the orientation process of specific populations. Withholding feedback from the field makes it very difficult to extract lessons and improve the model and the construction platform. Artificial intelligence technologies threaten many models today, so this model is no different.

The development process and the model are correct at the time of writing. The changing technologies and the fluctuating market will likely provide new information that will require us to confront it, ask the same questions again, and examine whether the model is successful or should be changed following the development of technology. The findings of the studies in the test case are promising but do not indicate the general rule. This does not mean that every case in the field of national security will carry the same results. Therefore, it is impossible to draw broad conclusions from specific projects. The model and platform must be considered a recommended outline and continue to ask many questions in managing the digital transformation process into virtual worlds.

4.3 SUGGESTIONS FOR FURTHER RESEARCH

The applied research presented here is the beginning of many studies that can be carried out based on the model and the software. The model and software can guide many test cases in any area of life, including medicine, tourism, gaming, aviation, the manufacturing industry, training, education, shopping, commerce, etc.

Relevant follow-up studies will examine the model's weak points and deficiencies, which I mentioned in the previous section on the study's limitations. It would be correct to examine whether the model's lack of a particular clause would harm its evaluation and the transformation process.

I recommend reviewing the model again every year and presenting recommendations for change and upgrade according to the state of technology and market readiness to consume solutions of virtual worlds. When the day comes when the platform will be mature enough to go out into the world for the end user, it will be correct to conduct a comprehensive study on the efficiency of the use of the software by the user and on the rate of growth in the number of regular users who testify to the advantages of the software compared to alternative processes. Also, retrospective research on projects will allow a relevant test of the platform's effectiveness since we can analyze the time and resources invested in about 100 projects and more. If we were to perform them today after the platform is established, how much time and resources would we save? Another study for the near future will address the differences between work groups, one of which will work with traditional methods for writing a strategy for digital transformation, and the other will work according to the model. A group of experts will examine the recommendations and will evaluate the ability to implement the projects. All the studies will deal with business questions. However, in the coming years, there will be a need to raise moral questions about collecting biometric information through technological devices.

4.4 APPLAY ARTIFICIAL INTELLIFENCE IN FURTHER RESEARCH

At the same time as the hype about the virtual worlds, there is an even bigger hype about artificial intelligence. In the world of generative AI and its natural connection to virtual worlds, there is potential for further research and ideas on how to integrate artificial intelligence into virtual worlds.

One of the applications is natural language processing, which can be combined with avatars to breathe life into them. The avatars can perform actions and serve as personal assistants for users, or they can even be service attendants in the store and help choose products and recommendations on demand.

Another combination of artificial intelligence can upgrade a prototype I have already created. It records the users and transfers voice to text. It analyzes the users according to their mood during the experience, speed of speech, and use of negative words. It evaluates the individual contribution to a social task.

The developing world of computer vision enables object recognition. Using an external tool for the virtual experience can combine engaging therapeutic experiences and create a human-machine interface that helps rehabilitation and treatment processes. Preliminary research is conducted in advanced processes in collaboration with the University of Haifa in Israel's Physiotherapy Department.

These days, prototypes of AI systems that produce generative three-dimensional objects are being released to the public. The ability to produce models through text can lead to tremendous resource savings. For each project these days, it is necessary to employ several modelers who build environments and interactive elements for the environments. This time can be shortened by hundreds of percent, thus producing solutions at a higher speed.

These are just the tip of the iceberg of AI possibilities combined with research in virtual worlds. Artificial intelligence is a powerful tool that strengthens every few months and produces better and more accurate processing. In the coming years, we will have a great interest in dealing with the question of the presence of artificial intelligence in the virtual worlds, and later it will become a necessity and an integral part of it.

5. REFERENCES

Adnan, M., & Anwar, K. (2020). Online Learning amid the COVID-19 Pandemic: Students' Perspectives. Online Submission, 2(1), 45-51.

Alabdulwahhab, F. A. (2018, April). Web 3.0: the decentralized web blockchain networks and protocol innovation. In 2018 1st International Conference on Computer Applications & Information Security (ICCAIS) (pp. 1-4). IEEE.

Alpala, L. O., Quiroga-Parra, D. J., Torres, J. C., & Peluffo-Ordóñez, D. H. (2022). Smart factory using virtual reality and online multi-user: Towards a metaverse for experimental frameworks. Applied Sciences, 12(12), 6258.

Alsop, T. Aug 23, 2022.Metaverse market revenue worldwide from 2021 to 2030. https://tinyurl.com/wkfhncpz

Andaluz, V. H., Sánchez, J. S., Sánchez, C. R., Quevedo, W. X., Varela, J., Morales, J. L., & Cuzco, G. (2018, June). Multi-user industrial training and education environment. In International Conference on Augmented Reality, Virtual Reality and Computer Graphics (pp. 533-546). Springer, Cham.

Ball, M. (2022). The metaverse: and how it will revolutionize everything. Liveright Publishing.

BOF insights. (october, 2022).Gen-Z and Fashion in the Age of Realism.
Bonifati, A., Guerrini, G., Lutz, C., Martens, W., Mazilu, L., Paton, N., ... & Zhou, Y. (2020). Holding a Conference Online and Live due to COVID-19. arXiv preprint arXiv:2004.07668.

Bowman, D. A., & McMahan, R. P. (2007). Virtual reality: how much immersion is enough?. Computer, 40(7), 36-43.

Breeding, M. (2006). Web 2.0? Let's get to Web 1.0 first. Computers in Libraries, 26(5), 30-33.

Brügger, N. (2009). Website history and the website as an object of study. New Media & Society, 11(1-2), 115-132.

Cambridge Dictionary. (2023). immersion definition.

https://tinyurl.com/pm5y4jw9 Chohan, U. W. (2022). Metaverse or Metacurse?. Available at SSRN.

Chris Stokel-Walker.(2020, September 3). Conferences bring large groups of people together to exchange ideas, network and do business. How can the industry ride out the Covid-19 era? [blog post]. Retrieved from: https://tinyurl.com/42b5u5b5

Clark, K.(September 23,2021).Luxury brand Moncler to host immersive digital fashion experience with Alicia Keys. https://tinyurl.com/3dxmp5zu

Clement , J. Apr 14, 2022. "Share of internet users in the United States who are interested in using the metaverse as of March 2022, by gender". https://tinyurl.com/tyy4c4uw

Cormode, G., & Krishnamurthy, B. (2008). Key differences between Web 1.0 and Web
2.0. First Monday.

Correia, A. P., Baran, E., & Yusop, F. D. (2007, June). Designing cross-border online collaborative learning experiences. In

EdMedia+ Innovate Learning (pp. 1769-1778). Association for the Advancement of Computing in Education (AACE).

Davis, R. C., & Pledger, J. (2022). Studying Aspects of Teamwork and Communication in a Virtual Reality Environment.

Demarinis, T. , Calligaro, L. , Harr, C. , & Mariani, J. (2018). Real learning in a virtual world. Deloitte insights. https://tinyurl.com/can429s5

Eckert, D., & Mower, A. (2020). The effectiveness of virtual reality soft skills training in the enterprise: a study.

García-Pereira, I., Vera, L., Aixendri, M. P., Portalés, C., & Casas, S. (2020). Multisensory experiences in virtual reality and augmented reality interaction paradigms. In Smart Systems Design, Applications, and Challenges (pp. 276-298). IGI Global.

Golosova, J., & Romanovs, A. (2018, November). The advantages and disadvantages of the blockchain technology. In 2018 IEEE 6th workshop on advances in information, electronic and electrical engineering (AIEEE) (pp. 1-6). IEEE.

Gonzalez-Franco, M., Perez-Marcos, D., Spanlang, B., & Slater, M. (2010, March). The contribution of real-time mirror reflections of motor actions on virtual body ownership in an immersive virtual environment. In 2010 IEEE virtual reality conference (VR) (pp. 111-114). IEEE.

Gray, L. M., Wong-Wylie, G., Rempel, G. R., & Cook, K. (2020). Expanding qualitative research interviewing strategies: Zoom video communications. The Qualitative Report, 25(5), 1292-1301.

Halabi, O. (2020). Immersive virtual reality to enforce teaching in engineering education. Multimedia Tools and Applications, 79(3), 2987-3004.

Harley, D. (2020). Palmer Luckey and the rise of contemporary virtual reality. Convergence, 26(5-6), 1144-1158.

Hoffman, H. G., Hollander, A., Schroder, K., Rousseau, S., & Furness, T. (1998). Physically touching and tasting virtual objects enhances the realism of virtual experiences. Virtual Reality, 3, 226-234. https://tinyurl.com/w76358ef https://tinyurl.com/bdebha9j

Junevičius, D. (2022). The history of stereoscopic photography in Lithuania from 1860 to 1915. III Jornadas sobre Investigación en Historia de la fotografía. La fotografía estereoscópica o en 3D, siglos XIX y XX, 151-159.

Kan, H. Y., Duffy, V. G., & Su, C. J. (2001). An Internet virtual reality collaborative environment for effective product design. Computers in Industry, 45(2), 197-213.

Kaulina, K., & Kaulins, G. (2018). Retargeting effects on consumer purchase intentions (Doctoral dissertation, Master Thesis) 09.12. 2019 tarihinde https://projekter. aau. dk/projekter/files/281242327/IM_thesis_Kristine_Kaulina_ _Girts_Kaulins. pdf adresinden erişildi).

Kerdvibulvech, C. (2022). Exploring the Impacts of COVID-19 on Digital and Metaverse Games. In International Conference on Human-Computer Interaction (pp. 561-565). Springer, Cham.

Kilteni, K., Groten, R., & Slater, M. (2012). The sense of embodiment in virtual reality. Presence: Teleoperators and Virtual Environments, 21(4), 373-387.

Kraus, S., Kanbach, D. K., Krysta, P. M., Steinhoff, M. M., & Tomini, N. (2022). Facebook and the creation of the metaverse: radical business model innovation or incremental transformation?. International Journal of Entrepreneurial Behavior & Research.

Lassoued, Z., Alhendawi, M., & Bashitialshaaer, R. (2020). An exploratory study of the obstacles for achieving quality in distance learning during the COVID-19 pandemic. Education Sciences, 10(9), 232.

Lehner, V. D., & DeFanti, T. A. (1997). Distributed virtual reality: Supporting remote collaboration in vehicle design. IEEE Computer Graphics and Applications, 17(2), 13-17.

Leotta, A., & Ross, M. (2018). Touring the 'World Picture': virtual reality and the tourist gaze. Studies in Documentary Film, 12(2),

150-162.

Li, R. C., Jung, S., McKee, R. D., Whitton, M. C., & Lindeman, R. W. (2021, November). Introduce Floor Vibration to Virtual Reality. In Proceedings of the 2021 ACM Symposium on Spatial User Interaction (pp. 1-2).

Liang, H. N., Lu, F., Shi, Y., Nanjappan, V., & Papangelis, K. (2019). Evaluating the effects of collaboration and competition in navigation tasks and spatial knowledge acquisition within virtual reality environments. Future Generation Computer Systems, 95, 855-866.

Liao, C. Y., Tai, S. K., Chen, R. C., & Hendry, H. (2020). Using EEG and deep learning to predict motion sickness under wearing a virtual reality device. IEEE Access, 8, 126784- 126796.

Lim, S., & Reeves, B. (2010). Computer agents versus avatars: Responses to interactive game characters controlled by a computer or other player. International Journal of Human-Computer Studies, 68(1-2), 57-68.

Marr, B. (22 Jun,2022).Forbes.The Metaverse And Digital Transformation At McDonald's. https://tinyurl.com/486fctfr

McGreevy, M. W. (1993). Virtual reality and planetary exploration. In Virtual Reality (pp. 163-197). Academic Press.

Mystakidis, S. (2022). Metaverse. Encyclopedia, 2(1), 486-497.

Nakamoto, T., Hirasawa, T., & Hanyu, Y. (2020, March). Virtual environment with smell using wearable olfactory display and computational fluid dynamics simulation. In 2020 IEEE Conference on Virtual Reality and 3D User Interfaces (VR) (pp.

713-720). IEEE.

Narin, N. G. (2021). A content analysis of the metaverse articles. Journal of Metaverse, 1(1), 17-24.

Niki, K., Yasui, M., Iguchi, M., Isono, T., Kageyama, H., & Ueda, M. (2021). A pilot study to develop a new method of assisting children in taking their medication by using immersive virtual reality. Biological and Pharmaceutical Bulletin, 44(2), 279-282.

Özcan, E. (2020). Analysis of Immersive Virtual Reality through Senses.

Paiva, P. V., Machado, L. S., Valença, A. M. G., Batista, T. V., & Moraes, R. M. (2018). SimCEC: a collaborative VR-based simulator for surgical teamwork education.
Computers in Entertainment (CIE), 16(2), 1-26.

Patil, K. (2021). A Study of Web 1.0 to 3.0. AGPE THE ROYAL GONDWANA RESEARCH JOURNAL OF HISTORY, SCIENCE, ECONOMIC, POLITICAL AND SOCIAL SCIENCE, 2(2), 40-45.

Pauna, H., Léger, P. M., Sénécal, S., Fredette, M., Courtemanche, F. Chen, S. L., ... & Ménard, J. F. (2018). The psychophysiological effect of a vibro-kinetic movie experience:
The case of the D-BOX movie seat.
In Information Systems and Neuroscience:
Gmunden Retreat on NeuroIS 2017 (pp. 1-7). Springer Internationa publishing.

Pepe, E., Bajardi, P., Gauvin, L., Privitera, F., Lake, B., Cattuto, C., & Tizzoni, M. (2020). COVID-19 outbreak response: a first assessment of mobility changes in Italy following national lockdown. MedRxiv.

Pérez, L., Rodríguez-Jiménez, S., Rodríguez, N., Usamentiaga, R., & García, D. F. (2020). Digital twin and virtual reality based methodology for multi-robot manufacturing cell commissioning. Applied sciences, 10(10), 3633.

Pollard, A. Nov 17, 2021. Gen Z has 30$ billion to spend, Trick is getting them to buy. https://tinyurl.com/42ehvwuy

Rakesh, R. (2018). Immersive learning for future workforce. Accenture. https://tinyurl.com/ycx4yubf

Ramic-Brkic, B., & Chalmers, A. (2010, June). Virtual smell: Authentic smell diffusion in virtual environments. In Proceedings of the 7th International Conference on Computer Graphics, Virtual Reality, Visualisation and Interaction in Africa (pp. 45-52).

Rana, A., Ozcinar, C., & Smolic, A. (2019, May). Towards generating ambisonics using audio-visual cue for virtual reality. In ICASSP 2019-2019 IEEE International Conference on Acoustics, Speech and Signal Processing (ICASSP) (pp. 2012-2016). IEEE.

Riva, G., Wiederhold, B., & Molinari, E. (1998). An investigation into factors influencing immersion in interactive virtual reality environments. In Virtual environments in clinical psychology and neuroscience (pp. 43-51). IOS.

Rudman, R., & Bruwer, R. (2016). Defining Web 3.0:

opportunities and challenges. The Electronic Library.

Ryan, M. L. (1999). Immersion vs. interactivity: Virtual reality and literary theory. SubStance, 28(2), 110-137.

S. Herz, R. (2021). Olfactory virtual reality: A new frontier in the treatment and prevention of posttraumatic stress disorder. Brain Sciences, 11(8), 1070.

Sanchez-Vives, M. V., & Slater, M. (2005). From presence to consciousness through virtual reality. Nature Reviews Neuroscience, 6(4), 332-339.

Shale, P.(August 11, 2022)The Omniverse – and the future of our virtual worlds.

Shamsuzzoha, A., Toshev, R., Vu Tuan, V., Kankaanpaa, T., & Helo, P. (2021). Digital factory–virtual reality environments for industrial training and maintenance. Interactive learning environments, 29(8), 1339-1362.

Sleeps, D. N. (2021). 8.0: https://www. domo.

com/learn/data-never-sleeps-8. Smith, W. R., Atala, A.

J., Terlecki, R. P., Kelly, E. E., & Matthews, C. A.

(2020).
Implementation guide for rapid integration of an outpatient telemedicine program
during the COVID-19 pandemic. Journal of the American College of Surgeons, 231(2), 216-222.

Start beyond.(n.d). https://tinyurl.com/2s3krnkz

Stone, R. J. (2001, July). Haptic feedback: A brief history from telepresence to virtual reality. In Haptic Human-Computer Interaction: First International Workshop Glasgow, UK, August 31—September 1, 2000 Proceedings (pp. 1-16). Berlin, Heidelberg: Springer Berlin Heidelberg.

SUTHERLAND, I. E. (2021, January). A head-mounted three dimensional display. 1968. In AFIPS Joint Computer Conferences Proceedings (Vol. 10, No. 1476589.1476686).

Taylor, S. (2005). People resourcing. CIPD Publishing.

Torrico, D. D., Han, Y., Sharma, C., Fuentes, S., Gonzalez Viejo, C., & Dunshea, F. R. (2020). Effects of context and virtual reality environments on the wine tasting experience, acceptability, and emotional responses of consumers. Foods, 9(2), 191.

Tubul-Lavy, z. Bianchi, s. virtual reality: new medium for training purposes. #netgame – next level education: gamification and digital teaching methods for the generation of today. RISR no.25,2021.

Wisniewski, A. (2019, May 31). The secret life of your nose: how to unlock your most primal sense. YouTube. https://tinyurl.com/3a844npr

Yang, J. T. (2007). The impact of knowledge sharing on organizational learning and effectiveness. Journal of knowledge management, 11(2), 83-90

Zackoff, M. W., Lin, L., Israel, K., Ely, K., Raab, D., Saupe, J., ... & Sitterding, M. (2020). The future of onboarding: implementation of immersive virtual reality for nursing clinical assessment training. Journal for Nurses in Professional Development, 36(4), 235-240.

Zackoff, M. W., Rios, M., Davis, D., Boyd, S., Roque, I., Anderson, I., ... & Moore, R. A. (2022). Immersive virtual reality onboarding using a digital twin for a new clinical space expansion: a novel approach to large-scale training for health care providers. The Journal of Pediatrics.

Zaker, R., & Coloma, E. (2018). Virtual reality-integrated workflow in BIM-enabled projects collaboration and design review: a case study. Visualization in Engineering, 6(1), 1-15.

APPENDIX - 5 I'S MODEL

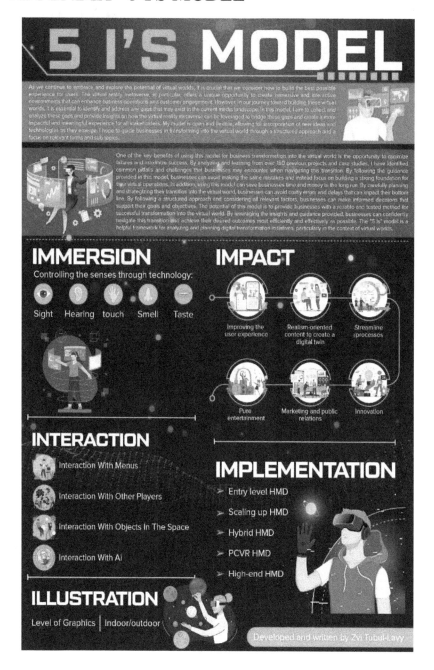